# How to Be a
# GROWN UP

### The Ten Secret Skills
### Everyone Needs to Know

## STACY KAISER

HarperOne
*An Imprint of HarperCollinsPublishers*

HarperOne

HarperCollins books may be purchased for educational, business, or sales promotional use. For information please write: Special Markets Department, Harper-Collins Publishers, 10 East 53rd Street, New York, NY 10022.

HarperCollins Web site: http://www.harpercollins.com

HarperCollins®, ▆®, and HarperOne™ are trademarks of HarperCollins Publishers.

FIRST EDITION

Designed by Janet M. Evans

Library of Congress Cataloging-in-Publication Data is available.

ISBN: 978-0-06-194118-4

10 11 12 13 14 RRD(H) 10 9 8 7 6 5 4 3 2 1

To my daughters Jordan and Katie:
I am the luckiest mom in the world.
You are both beautiful inside and out.

# CONTENTS

**I never wanted** to be a therapist, a counselor, or even a "relationship expert." I have always been quite content being a comedian, so when *He's Just Not That Into You*, the book I coauthored, caught on, suddenly thousands of people were turning to me for advice on their own relationships. My strong suits are my opinion and my ability to offer some essential truths, particularly about men, women, and dating, in a candid but entertaining way. I have no formal training in counseling people. Even so, I was given my own talk show, where I was expected to give advice for an hour every day on a wide variety of topics, and do so with authority. Clearly, I was in over my head.

Enter Stacy Kaiser! One day we assembled a panel of experts; for some reason Stacy was in another room in the studio and on a monitor on the set. I guess we were trying to pretend we had a satellite hookup. Despite the cockamamie setup, Stacy was the brightest light on the stage! She was foxy, smart, intuitive, and made for all-around great television. I said to my producers, "That girl should have her own show. Do you think we could get her to be a regular?" And thus began my relationship with this extraordinary person.

Stacy became the professional, therapeutic voice of our show. And if you were one of the eight people who watched it, you remember how good she is at taking an issue, breaking it down into its simplest pieces, and making big problems not only understandable, but more important, conquerable. Stacy tackles hard subjects, but not in a hard way. She is a strong believer in everyone's ability to grow and change, and she genuinely wants to help people enjoy worthwhile lives. She accompanies her straightforward advice with a big dose of understanding and encouragement.

Stacy and I share the belief that *you* are in control of your own happiness, and it really comes down to making better choices to support that goal. Figuring out what those choices are is the hard part. The ability to act in your own long-term best interest is one thing that differentiates children from adults. In fact, that's what being a real grown up is: making the smart (though sometimes difficult) choices while refusing to fall into negative self-defeating traps. Stacy has now brought you all of her best information on making these choices and, with this book, can help you learn how to do just that.

*How to Be a Grown Up* has been too long in coming, and it's a book I wish I'd had earlier in life. Stacy narrows daily life, and its roadblocks, down to its core elements. By exposing any underlying issues and offering practical solutions and support, she makes it achievable for anyone to make lasting changes in their existing behaviors—at least the ones that are keeping you from the kind of life you deserve to have! I particularly enjoyed what she has to say on the subject of "grown-up love." However, whether it's stress and overload, your appearance, addiction, money problems—whatever your issue may be—she has it covered.

Stacy Kaiser is a therapist, a counselor, and a relationship expert. I know this from firsthand experience. You see, she is the real deal. She doesn't do her work because she wants to be famous or on television. She truly believes she can help people. In lieu of telling you a long dull story about my life, let me just say that her advice changed my way of thinking. Most important, she was instrumental in making me see the value in my own work. So do me, and more important yourself, a favor. Take the quiz, read the book, and get on the path toward living the life you came here to live—as a real grown up!

—GREG BEHRENDT

# Introduction

**A**s a therapist who has counseled thousands of people over the last twenty years, I have heard all kinds of stories about the struggles people face in life. While every person is unique, and the details and circumstances of the problems each one faces vary, I have noticed a common theme that often emerges in our conversations. The challenge we grown ups have is to effectively balance the desire for fun and freedom against our responsibilities. Many of the people I see have had entirely too much fun and freedom. They spent money they didn't have, skipped work or were late once too often, acted rashly and tossed away a valuable relationship, regret how they raised their children, or put a quick thrill above an important obligation. Often, a crisis or emotional dilemma brings these people to the realization that they need to regroup and take on some adult priorities and responsibilities.

The other kind of people I often run into have the overly conscientious, type A, got-to-have-it-all-and-be-perfect kind of personality. These men and women white-knuckle it all the way through life. They exhaust themselves trying to obtain the ideal house, mate, job, and children. They are overscheduled every minute of every day. They rarely have any fun and have no idea how to relax. They don't have date nights or time off with their friends or joke around at the office. It's all work, business, responsibility, worries, and getting ahead. They lack any sense of freedom! No matter what monetary success these people achieve, they often wind up unhappy, longing for connection, wishing for the ability to let their hair down, and wondering if this is all there is.

Personally, I have learned firsthand the satisfaction of achieving a balance in my life between my many responsibilities and freedom and fun. I made a conscious decision years ago that I wanted to live what I call a fully loaded grown-up life! By that I mean that when I'm eighty years old, playing shuffleboard somewhere, I want to be able to look back and say my life turned out pretty much the way I wanted it to. I was responsible and helped people and took good care of my family and had a fulfilling career, but I also had a great time enjoying all the benefits and fun times this world has to offer!

I'm sure you've heard the saying "You can have it all—just not at the same time." I agree. This book is not about getting it all instantly. It is about maximizing your potential and thus maximizing your chances for happiness and success. In the quiz offered in chapter 1 and in the chapters that follow, you will learn how to balance your time and resources for fun and freedom while taking care of your responsibilities, all while managing a full and busy life.

My intent in this book is to challenge you. I am going to encourage you to examine who you truly are and what you want out of life, and I'll show you that being a true grown up is a very desirable state. Maybe you are aware of areas in your life that could stand some shoring up and you are exploring options to conduct your life a little differently while adapting more peacefully to its difficulties. This book will give you the tools and skills you need to take you to the next level.

You've made a very grown-up decision already—to begin the journey not only toward knowing yourself better but creating the life you've always wanted!

# 1

# The Quiz

**I** remember, as a kid, wanting so badly to be a "grown up." I couldn't wait till I was an adult, because once I was, I was convinced, I'd be free. I wouldn't have to go to bed when I was told. I would buy myself any toy I liked on the spot. No one could tell me what to eat, so I could stuff myself with junk food. I would decide which TV shows were "appropriate" for me to watch. I would do my homework if and when I felt like it, and no one would ever make me clean up my room. Bottom line: I'd do what I liked, and I would be happy.

So, here I am, and so are you. We've arrived; we are officially adults. Chronological grown ups who are free to live our lives any way we want to. Right? Well, sort of. Although we are free to make our own choices, we find ourselves still bound by all kinds of rules, boundaries, and expectations. Some we set for ourselves; many are imposed on us by friends, family, bosses, coworkers, mates, society, and the world around us. The big catch is that with freedom comes responsibility. A real grown up knows how to balance the two.

For better or worse, now you're completely in charge of your own life. You get to decide what to eat, how much to sleep, who to date or marry, where to work, whether to be fat or thin, whether to dress conservatively or seductively, how much money to spend, how to raise your children, and so much more. So how's everything going—great? Are you enjoying a rewarding, well-paid job and fulfilling relationships with friends, family, and coworkers? Is there romantic love in your life? Are you addiction free? In good health? At peace with your appearance and body? Are your finances solid? Are you pleased about the progress you've made so far in achieving your hopes and dreams and excited about what's coming next in your life?

If everything is going exactly as you'd like, congratulations! You are in a rare and wonderful position and may feel that you already know how to be a grown up. But if you feel like some things are missing, that you are not in complete control of your life, or that you lack some of the skills and tools to live the life you long for, then I am certain this book will change your life.

Being smart and self-aware enough to own up to the fact that there may be some areas where you need to grow up is certainly the first step. The next step involves putting your finger on exactly what is blocking your path and figuring out how to fix it. Over the years I have identified what I consider to be the ten critical areas a person needs to address in order to be a successful, happy, high-functioning adult. Problems in any one of these areas can lead to the numerous pitfalls that prevent you from living the life you dream of. Whatever challenges you are facing (or have so far been unwilling to face)—whether that means being overweight or unable to get along with your mother or being consistently underemployed—can be traced back to one or more of these ten overall areas.

You must become consciously aware of the patterns of behavior and traits—positive and negative—that have either rewarded you or are holding you back. Once you've determined your initial trouble spots, you'll have the power to learn and change. This is where I come in. I have worked with thousands of people just like you, who are facing a roadblock in life or simply want more than they currently have. I strongly believe that as you embark on a journey to expand your knowledge of yourself and improve your life, you must begin with an acknowledgment of any baggage and an awareness of how it impacts you today. I'm going to talk about baggage frequently throughout this book, so let's define what I mean.

## Baggage: Is Yours Small Enough to Fit in the Overhead Bin?

We all travel through life with baggage. Some of us carry a compact bag small enough to fit in the overhead compartment or under the seat. Others carry a full set of Louis Vuitton . . . equipped with a large trunk, medium rolling bag, and small pieces with tiny compartments in which to hide even the tiniest of items. Now, I'm guessing you may realize that I am not talking about luggage that you'd borrow from a friend or buy in a store or online. I'm talking about the kind of baggage we carry with us every day—even when we don't know it's there. Baggage evolves from painful, harmful, or negative experiences and from interactions that caused a significant emotional reaction within you. These feelings continue to shape who you are, how you think, the choices you make, and the actions you take now. Baggage will impair your ability to function, adapt, and evolve.

There are two main types of baggage: the baggage you see and are well aware of, and the baggage you don't see and aren't aware of. The baggage you see but choose not to acknowledge or unload can be dangerous. Your choice to ignore it and not deal with it means that for some reason you are *allowing* it to interfere with your life, your relationships, and your future. The baggage you don't see and may not even be aware of is equally dangerous, because it can sneak up on you and ambush you out of nowhere, and if you don't see something coming, how can you manage it, control it, or change it?

Now, if you are reading this and thinking that you are quite aware of all your baggage and you feel that it is manageable enough to carry on your life journey without any burden, great! You've got a head start toward maximizing your potential. But what if you didn't even realize the load you are carrying until you read about it here? Or what if your baggage keeps getting in your way and you don't know how to fix it? What if your past keeps impacting your present on a regular basis? If you are experiencing any of these issues, then know that simply becoming aware of your baggage and its impact is the first step toward beginning to let some of it go.

The interesting thing about excess baggage is that it seems to become almost comfortable to carry. It's as if you become so used to walking around carrying this extra weight that you don't realize how much more you could see and do in life if you were carrying a lighter load. It's like hiking with a twenty-pound backpack or carrying an armful of shopping bags through the mall. You know you've got the extra burden, but you don't realize how much lighter you could feel until you put the backpack or bags down.

This hidden baggage is the baggage you hide from the world and sometimes even from yourself. It's like that twenty-dollar bill you slip into an old purse or pair of pants that you hope to forget about but are surprised to find later! Baggage can trick you into believing things such as: the relationship with the person who is just like your father is okay because "you're used to it" and "you can handle it." It can cause you to tolerate a job that works you a million hours for low pay and no appreciation, and yet you stay because you are used to working your fingers to the bone and getting nothing in return. It might lead you to stay close to a self-centered friend who talks your ear off, but you've "always been quiet anyway." Do you ever hear yourself making similar comments? These examples reflect what I call "hidden baggage experiences."

Whether it's excess or hidden baggage, it's weighing you down, getting in your way, and causing you to bend and twist out of shape trying to be flexible enough to adapt. This phenomenon is best explained by the story of the frog in boiling water.

Do you know what happens to a frog if you put it into a pot of cold water and slowly turn up the heat until the water eventually boils? The frog acclimates and continues to acclimate until eventually it explodes. Excess baggage and hidden baggage create these types of explosions in us. They keep us perpetuating experiences and feelings that we have had before because they are familiar and we have grown used to them; we acclimate.

Baggage is driven by negative emotions such as anger, fear, and sadness. The feelings are based in: "How did I end up like this?" "It's not my fault, so how can I fix it, or why should I fix it?" "My life isn't fair; things like this always happen to me"; and "I can do what I want because my life has been rough." These underlying feelings can lead to a desire to act out or remain passive due to feelings of helplessness or hopelessness.

I am here to tell you that power comes from knowing where your baggage stems from and asking yourself the following critical questions: Assuming I can choose to behave any way I want, do I like the way I am behaving? Should I or others have to suffer because of my past? Can I manage painful or uncomfortable emotions by committing to behaving differently?

If your baggage is the result of traumatic experiences like physical or sexual abuse, being victimized in a crime, or being injured in a horrible car crash, this book won't be enough, and you should consider talking with a professional about processing that experience.

For the rest of us who are carrying lighter yet still burdensome loads, a good start toward addressing baggage is to have a present-day reality check. When your immediate reaction to an experience is anger, fear, or sadness, STOP. Analyze this feeling. Ask yourself: am I upset (or fearful, or humiliated, or shocked) by what just happened or what someone said because it is significant in my life now, or have these words or actions triggered something from my past that will cause me to feel or react way out of proportion to what actually occurred today?

I often suggest to people I counsel that they turn their inner baggage into outer baggage. To do that, make a list of the critical ways your baggage has impacted you. Write down things like: I was neglected as a child, so I have chosen relationships where I am neglected; or my parents escaped from pain by overindulging in food/alcohol/drugs, and I do the same; or I have always feared failing, so I don't put my best effort forward with my family, friends or job. Take this list of inner baggage and put it in your purse, backpack, or briefcase. Carry it wherever you go—I mean, you do anyway—only this time carry it on paper to remind you of where it all came from.

## Moving Forward

So here's what I need from you. You agree to take responsibility for making the necessary changes in your thought patterns and behavior and work toward making improvements in the areas that need enhancement—after all, it is your life! Try as you might, you will never be able to control anyone's actions but your own, so the challenge to you in this book is to commit to focusing on and improving your own life—with my help, of course!

Imagine the benefits that will be yours as a fully loaded grown up: You'll be able to handle your responsibilities and feel in control of your own life. You'll be motivated to become an action-oriented person, someone who is able to initiate change instead of just reacting to events. You'll be well prepared to bounce back from setbacks and disappointments. Best of all, you will enjoy true freedom, not the kind you envisioned as a child, meaning eating ice cream for dinner, but the confidence that you are capable of living your own best life and reaching your unique destiny.

## THE QUIZ

Let's begin by getting clear about what's really going on inside of you. The questions in the quiz on the following pages cover ten crucial life areas and are designed to give you an opportunity to reflect on your life right now, so you can then decide where you should concentrate your efforts for growth and change. Now I hope you plan to read this book in its entirety, as all these life areas integrate and overlap, but I imagine certain questions or concerns will resonate more strongly than others. If particular questions strike a chord—and more likely than not, you are already aware of some areas where you need a bit of help—then you will have a good sense of which chapters to pay particularly close attention to.

When everything is humming along smoothly in these ten areas, your life should be fantastic. If you can answer all of these questions the way you'd like to without a feeling of self-doubt, then you have achieved my definition of being a fully loaded grown up. But if you are unable to do that (and, no, this doesn't go on your permanent record!), then we immediately know where the pressing challenges lie. Childhood issues,

earning potential, financial responsibility, intimate relationships—by considering these questions you'll be able to pin-
point what is keeping you from satisfaction and fulfillment.

**DIRECTIONS:** Answer each question either TRUE or
FALSE. Don't overthink the question; just go with your immediate gut reaction to it. Each answer is assigned a certain
point value. At the end of the quiz, add up your score for a
total. There are a total of 270 possible points; the higher your
score, the closer you are to being a fully loaded grown up!

Recalling and discussing past relationships is upsetting to me.

True: 0     False: 3

I am unaware of the details of my finances—my spouse, parent, or
business partner handles that.

True: 0     False: 5

I look appealing enough to attract a mate or feel appealing enough to
be desirable to my current mate.

True: 4     False: 0

I tend to buy what I want now and worry about paying the bill later.

True: 0     False: 4

I believe I was meant to do something completely different from what I
currently do for a living.

True: 0     False: 3

I make time to nurture the relationships I have.

True: 5     False: 0

I am usually running behind, but it's no big deal.

> True: 0          False: 3

I am over the age of twenty-one and completely financially dependent on another person.

> True: 0          False: 5

I believe I will live with an addiction forever because I don't have the strength or desire to be free of it.

> True: 0          False: 5

I equate money or gifts with love.

> True: 0          False: 4

I am uncomfortable expressing my feelings.

> True: 0          False: 4

I am willing to do my part to improve the relationships in my life.

> True: 5          False: 0

I secretly believe that I have not accomplished as much as or more than my peers, friends, and family members.

> True: 0          False: 3

I look ahead, plan, visualize, and set goals for my future.

> True: 4          False: 0

I am very affected by criticism and setbacks that others easily brush off.

> True: 0          False: 3

I bury my personal troubles in work.

> True: 1          False: 3

I express my emotions appropriately and rarely resort to screaming, cursing, blaming others, or hiding.

True: 4     False: 0

I am currently or am frequently jobless/laid off/unemployed.

True: 0     False: 5

I can easily list the top ten characteristics and traits that I am looking for or have found in a mate.

True: 3     False: 0

I regularly use mood-altering substances or activities to help me relax.

True: 0     False: 5

My health has suffered due to addictive substances or behaviors (smoking, alcoholism, obesity, anorexia, drugs)

True: 0     False: 4

I feel compelled to live above my means to keep up with my friends in terms of cars, houses, and clothing.

True: 0     False: 4

I know a lot of details about my friends' and family's lives, and they know a lot about mine.

True: 3     False: 0

I rarely feel out of control.

True: 3     False: 1

I have lost jobs or strained relationships because of my behavior and actions.

True: 0     False: 5

I would say that I am addicted to my iPhone, the Internet, Facebook, texting, etc.

$$\text{True: } 0 \qquad \text{False: } 2$$

I am invested in solving my own problems and not relying on other people for help.

$$\text{True: } 4 \qquad \text{False: } 2$$

I feel out of control and anxious when I think about my financial future.

$$\text{True: } 0 \qquad \text{False: } 3$$

I am generally satisfied with my appearance.

$$\text{True: } 5 \qquad \text{False: } 0$$

I have been forced to borrow money more than once from friends or family members.

$$\text{True: } 0 \qquad \text{False: } 3$$

I frequently clash with my boss and coworkers.

$$\text{True: } 0 \qquad \text{False: } 5$$

I tend to isolate myself when times get tough.

$$\text{True: } 0 \qquad \text{False: } 3$$

When something bothers me about my appearance, I take action to improve it or learn to accept it.

$$\text{True: } 4 \qquad \text{False: } 0$$

Financial stability is the most important trait in a partner to me.

$$\text{True: } 2 \qquad \text{False: } 2$$

When I shop for clothes, I don't need others' opinions; I know exactly what to buy that's right for my body and lifestyle.

True: 4     False: 2

I pay attention to eating well and practicing healthy habits on a daily basis.

True: 5     False: 0

I personally know at least three couples I consider role models of relationships I'd like to emulate in my own life.

True: 3     False: 2

I have recognized and broken many harmful patterns in my life.

True: 5     False: 0

When someone compliments my appearance, I trust that the person is sincere.

True: 3     False: 0

I have an emergency financial plan in place if I lose my job.

True: 5     False: 0

I frequently buy items I don't need.

True: 0     False: 4

I excel at caring for others but feel unable to ask for help for myself when I need it.

True: 2     False: 4

I have poor money-management skills.

True: 0     False: 5

Friends tease me about being cheap.

True: 0     False: 2

I prefer to connect with others using technology—phone, computer, IM—rather than face-to-face.

True: 0     False: 2

I struggle with issues that are clearly visible to strangers (morbid obesity, anorexia, depression, anxiety).

True: 0     False: 5

I tend to stay too long in dysfunctional or abusive relationships in my business or personal life.

True: 0     False: 5

My job pays the bills but does not fulfill me or give me a sense of accomplishment.

True: 3     False: 4

I am able to fairly and calmly address and confront family members and friends on inappropriate behavior and remarks directed to me.

True: 5     False: 0

I have been cautioned by well-meaning friends or family members that I have a drinking/smoking/overeating problem.

True: 0     False: 5

I become easily overwhelmed when I feel that too many demands are being made of me.

True: 0     False: 4

I have confidence in my ability to be in charge of my own life and make the best decisions for myself.

True: 5     False: 0

I frequently run out of cash before my next paycheck arrives.

True: 0     False: 4

I have had a satisfying intimate relationship in my lifetime.

True: 4     False: 0

I don't need to manage my own life, because I have found others to do that for me.

True: 0     False: 5

There are many people in my life who frown on the way I behave.

True: 0     False: 5

I am able to balance what I have to do (work, family, chores) with what I want to do.

True: 5     False: 0

I have great difficulty trusting the motivations of other people.

True: 0     False: 3

I feel that I don't truly fit in or belong anywhere.

True: 0     False: 4

I have a hard time maintaining long-term friendships and making new friends.

True: 0     False: 4

I am confident that I can count on my family for help, and they can count on me.

True: 3      False: 0

I feel I must put up a strong front and refuse to show weakness to others, even my friends.

True: 1      False: 4

I ask for what I want and need in a relationship in a productive way.

True: 5      False: 0

I believe all my problems could be solved if I had more money.

True: 1      False: 2

My ego and sense of self-worth is completely tied up in my title (doctor, professor, vice president).

True: 0      False: 3

I am capable and confident about my sexuality.

True: 5      False: 0

I set and follow through on long-term goals.

True: 5      False: 0

I make regular sleep and exercise priorities.

True: 4      False: 0

# 2

# Talk Is Cheap...
# Communication,
# Priceless

**O**ur first act of communication took place when we moved around and kicked in the womb—as if to announce, "I'm here!" Ask any woman who has ever been pregnant—she will immediately recall her delight at the sensation of receiving that first message from her unborn child. When we are born, we cry. Our first verbal communication with the world says "It's cold, and the lights are too bright!" From our first breath we are trying to communicate: I am here. I exist. These are the same fundamental desires we all carry with us throughout our entire lifetimes.

Our parents and caregivers spend the first months of our lives trying desperately to understand what it is we are trying to communicate. Are we hungry? Wet? Tired? If our caregivers are attentive and tenacious, they begin to understand what we want and need long before we can ever utter a word. They learn to know what we are saying when we turn our faces and pull away from the bottle when we're full. We reach for our favorite toys. We stare in fascination at our reflection in a mirror. We smile when we taste our first bite of ice cream! There's no need to talk. It is this comprehension and meeting of our needs that forms the foundation of our ability to effectively express ourselves. As we grow, our caregivers help us refine the way we ask for things and hopefully give us the right amount of things, explain why the answer is no sometimes, withhold certain things, and stick firmly to no when it's necessary. In other words, they communicate clearly, and we learn to balance our needs and wants and how best to achieve them.

These are the characteristics of an ideal caregiver, but the reality is that few of us were fortunate enough to have ideal caregivers as children. Some of us had siblings; our parents were rushed, busy, working, and stressed about finances, health, or even daily life so they couldn't always attend to us. On the other end of the spectrum, we might have been an only child, the light of someone's life, pampered and spoiled and overindulged. Every child learns to communicate in his or her own unique situation. As kids, we demand and react. As teenagers, we push boundaries and act out, and higher thinking and advanced communication skills come into play as we learn to negotiate with our parents, friends, and teachers.

Typically, whatever environment we grow up in affects us in one of two predictable ways. We either mimic exactly what we learned at our parents' feet or do just the opposite. If you grew up in a household of screamers, you might either be a screamer yourself or a timid little mouse who never asks for anything. If your parent is pushy and demanding, there's a good chance you will become a pushy, demanding adult—or go the other way and be a doormat who asks for and gets very little. If the members of your family examine and dissect every topic incessantly, you will likely become a big talker—or you'll be quiet and prefer to keep your thoughts to yourself. Some parents encourage openness and frank discussion of problems; others ignore everything and maintain secrets and silence. Because your childhood influences have everything to do with how you communicate with people today, it's important to realize who you are and where you came from.

Along the way your communication style becomes influenced by your friends, bosses, coworkers, and many of the people you interact with. As an adult, you have probably settled on a communication style that is comfortable for you. I am guessing that most people reading this book are pretty good communicators already. What I want to discuss is going from good to great—from being a reasonably effective communicator to a person who excels in dynamic interaction! That means fully loaded, maximum-capacity mastery of all the bigger elements of communication so that you can achieve your highest level of success!

Dynamic communication is an ever-evolving art. It also happens to be one of the easiest areas to change and fix. Once you get past the baseline of basic talking, everything else can be learned and practiced and improved upon over your entire life. If you practice these skills enough, they will become an automatic part of who you are. Dynamic interacters are more thoughtful; they have very little conflict in their lives, and they get more of what they want out of every situation and relationship because they've mastered how to get it! Now, doesn't that sound appealing?

## Responding Consciously

Imagine that you live alone or that you come home one day knowing that everyone else in your family is out. It's nighttime, it's dark, and when you reach the front door, you hear a noise inside. What might you be thinking? *There's an intruder inside*, or *What could that be?* What might you be feeling? Probably scared, mad, or worried. The communication you'd be having with yourself at that point would be a reaction to those feelings. In response, you might call the police, or you might open the door and shout, "Who's there?" You might go knock on a neighbor's door and ask him to accompany you inside. All because you're operating under the assumption that someone is inside your house who's not supposed to be there.

Let's take the same scenario—nighttime, dark, you're not expecting anyone to be home. All of a sudden you run into a friend on your sidewalk who says, "Oh my gosh! You weren't supposed to see me! There's a surprise inside; pretend this never happened!" and runs off. Now as you approach the door and hear a noise, what are you thinking? *Oh, there's a party for me inside!* or *I'm not dressed right!* How do you feel? Excited, apprehensive, maybe worried about how to fake surprise. Your response to the same initial scenario is happy!

What ultimately comes out of you has everything to do with the thoughts and feelings going on inside of you. You should slow down and gather as much information as possible before responding. The more information you have, the more accurate and well received your communication will be. Take a few seconds to think about how you want to come across when you reply, what you want to say, and the feelings you want to convey. It's simply about taking a few extra seconds to process all the available information so you can respond appropriately to the situation.

## Voices

Most people would describe communication as how they interact with other people. I'd like you to give some thought to what I consider the foundation of dynamic interaction, which can be summed up in one simple question: how do you talk to yourself? We all have voices constantly chattering inside our heads—and I don't mean the kind that require intervention and medication! I am referring to the ongoing running commentary that accompanies us all as we go about our lives. These voices might be approving, harsh, judgmental, or sending us reminders and warnings—it all depends on who we are with and what we're doing. I want you to become more conscious of these voices, and remember: the first and most important person we communicate with is ourselves.

Let's take a common scenario among single people: You're at a party where you've met somebody you're interested in dating, and you've spent a couple of hours chatting with this fantastic person. One voice in your head exults, *This person's so great, I can't believe the chemistry, we get along so well,* while another voice inside warns, *Danger! You might get rejected. You always get dumped, you're a loser, you'll never find a good relationship.* Meanwhile the warnings of your parents echo in your mind: *You're going to wind up alone!* or *You can afford to be picky, you're perfect!* There's so much noise going on inside your head that you don't know what to do or how to act!

The grown-up response is to isolate and identify those voices. They all come from one of three places:

Your past: your history and your baggage

Your slippery slope "fantasy" voice

The voice of reason and reality

These voices crowd our heads in many situations, but particularly in romantic relationships. The past history voice might say to you: *this will never work out, nobody ever stays with me, I always get dumped, I always pick losers.* This voice is screaming all kinds of warnings at you, based on your baggage and history. It is jumping way ahead in your imagination and already picturing this person cheating on you. I have had clients who have imagined an entire lurid scenario about a relationship because a partner didn't pick up his phone one night!

Then you have your fantasy voice, the one that imagines in the most glowing or most traumatic terms what could happen. It seizes on a few small inconsequential remarks and runs wildly away! This is the voice that starts planning a wedding on the first date and picturing the two of you in a cute little house with a picket fence. Or it's your first day of work in the mailroom, and you're imagining yourself running the company or, conversely, getting fired that afternoon. You meet an interesting colleague at a function and immediately think, *We're going to be best friends!* or *I know he/she will never like me!* When you give these voices too much credence, you run the risk of assuming and asking for too much too soon or missing out on something that could be really wonderful—and neither is an ideal outcome.

The grown-up voice is the voice of reason and reality. Often, this voice gets drowned out among the other two voices. The grown-up voice says, *this is a new person or situation. I will listen carefully to what's being said and do my best to respond to what is actually occurring in this exchange—not allowing events that happened in the past or any negative fantasies of the future to affect me.* The grown-up voice also serves as a guide. It may say to you: *based on my previous interactions with this acquaintance/boss/customer/good friend, he or she responds best to this tone . . . I'd better avoid this topic . . . We always enjoy discussing that . . . I can get what I want in this negotiation this way.* The grown-up voice is the one you need to listen to for important decisions and accurate guidance. This is how to hear it:

*Take a few seconds* to determine which thoughts or voices are running through your head, reflecting either of the two extremes—your past baggage or the fantasy voice— the good and the bad.

*Concentrate on the voice of reality.* Figure out what's really happening. This really is your first day on the job! What's really happening is you met an attractive person at a friend's party. What's really happening is you had one great conversation with a nice person at a business lunch. Figure out what's really going on, so you can figure out how to respond! Then you can be a dynamic interacter!

*Find a reliable mirror.* A mirror is a person who will give you honest and accurate feedback about how you look, what you say, and how you behave. We are going to speak a great deal in this book about the importance of surrounding yourself with the best possible support system. A reliable mirror, in the form of a reasonably impartial person, whether that's a coworker or a particularly sensible friend, is a necessity in our lives when we need a check on our self-communication skills. When you go on one promising date or have a fantastic job interview, it's great to call a good friend and rave on and on. "I think this is the one; we're going to get married!" Or, "They loved me; I'll be running that place in no time!"

Here's where the "reliable" part comes in. "I totally think you should get married, you both live in the same neighborhood, and you both like wine . . . it's perfect!" Friends mean well, but they can feed the fire of an overzealous imagination and reinforce the fantasy voice, for better or worse. Friends who know you well can be an unnecessary downer. Maybe they say, after the first date or interview when you haven't heard anything, "He (or they) didn't like you. Move on," when there could be a million other reasons why you haven't heard back. Or you may be annoyed at your mate or boss, call a friend to complain a bit, and she will say, "Yeah, remember when he did this? And this . . . remember that time he said this about you?" This will greatly impact how you handle your next communication with that person. Don't let others, even good friends, unduly influence these voices. The whole purpose of a mirror is to give you a real-life reflection.

All of this endless, ongoing internal dialogue is normal, of course. All these conflicting voices and impulses are what make us human and unpredictable. But it's a real grown up who slows down and gathers real evidence. Dynamic communication means listening to your grown-up voice, checking your reactions, if necessary, with a reliable mirror, and refusing to allow your past history and negative fantasy voices to influence your behavior.

**Now that we've covered communicating with yourself, let's move on** to what most people call communication: how you deal with others. Dynamic interaction involves the ability to get other people to be impacted by your communication. It's like a teeter-totter: if one person suddenly shifts the way she teeters, the other person must change the way she totters. The way you are communicating with any particular person can change quickly. If I soften my voice, it will most likely defuse a tense conversation. If I get louder or start to yell, it can immediately cause the other person to escalate and yell back—or back down, possibly thinking that I'm a crazy person. If I listen more empathetically, the other person may open up. If I dominate the conversation, it may make the other person speak less.

When I was in school, working as a waitress, I was surprised at how much my mood affected my tips. I've since heard the same thing from people who work in sales. If you're having a good day and feeling happy, you will communicate that attitude to the world. On a good day you'll get bigger tips and make more sales, and everyone will respond more positively toward you. If you are communicating feelings of anger and upset, you will not fare nearly as well.

## Stumbling Blocks to
## Dynamic Communication

Something I've noticed in years of counseling clients is that a common hindrance to dynamic interaction is the need to be right. What is more important when it comes to interacting with your family, boss, coworkers, or mate—being close, connected, and respecting who you are speaking to, or being right? That's a key factor when it comes to being a grown up. You have to care more about the long-term outcome than you do about the immediate gratification of being heard, being louder, winning, getting the last word, or being right.

The need to be right—which turns many a discussion into heated conflict—typically stems either from an overinflated sense of pride—you are overly invested in always being right—or it comes from a place of insecurity. You may worry that if you are not viewed as right in every situation, you will be considered stupid or inadequate or incapable. If I'm walking into a situation where I feel outmatched and worry that people might think I'm beneath them, I'm going in with my walls up, keeping my pride intact, and will not be able to communicate in a way that benefits us all.

A dynamic communicator lets go of the need to win. The real winning comes from a successful relationship, not scoring points. You want to win the war, not fight endless battles. At the end of the day, dynamic interaction leaves both people walking away feeling satisfied or happy. One or both may have compromised during the process, but neither is walking away upset, hurt, or feeling that he got short shrift.

Life, unfortunately, is full of intense, high-drama situations where even the best communicators are put to the test—not to mention the small, day-to-day annoyances such as rude waiters, indifferent salespeople, and sarcastic coworkers. Dynamic communicators do their best to keep themselves—and others—in check. Yes, occasionally they may scream, they may lose it, they may say the wrong thing. But 90 percent of the time, they won't. They'll walk away, they'll apologize, they'll take the higher road for the higher good.

Poor communicators run the gamut from mean or inappropriate to verbally abusive and critical. Being a grown up means setting the boundary, even if you only do so in your mind. Some people are shattered by criticism or mean remarks, instead of calmly saying, "That hurt my feelings. What are you so angry about?" or something similar, the hurt person says nothing, slinks home, and broods for days, weeks, or even years about it. If this is you, it's time for a reality check. It is never too late to take ownership of solving your own problems communicating!

There are a variety of ways to handle difficult and upsetting people and situations. Two less-than-grown-up ways are: You retreat and no longer communicate with the person at all, which sends a clear message—I'm not speaking to you. Or you brood and then later call and yell at the offender—also getting your message across.

A more effective way might be a joking method: "I guess I only told you seven hundred times that I don't want you to do this . . . so here's reminder seven hundred and one. Clearly, I didn't tell you enough times."

I find the "put it on yourself" method effective. Say something like, "You know, I don't know what's wrong with me . . . I keep stressing that I don't want to get involved in this, and everybody keeps trying to draw me in. I'm having a real problem; I'm upset that I'm not getting through. I need your help."

Direct but polite is what I call "relationship maintenance." Say something like, "You know, I've noticed that you tend to . . . I'm just wondering if people get angry with you about that, because I was certainly annoyed with you the other day."

There are many ways to handle these situations, but it all starts with you. Everybody tends to believe that personal problems have something to do with other people. "They're mean." "He said that . . . , so I said this!" Ultimately, it all has to do with you. Who are you; what kind of person do you want to be in the world; how do you want other people to see you; what do you want to get out of an interaction? What I recommend that clients do is get clear about what they want out of every relationship they have.

What kind of employee do you want to be? Do you want to be the boss? Do you want your coworkers to fear and be intimidated by you, or like you? Do you want to be a team player, or do you only want to look out for yourself? Do you want to be a quiet, nurturing friend who is always there to listen and help, or do you enjoy being the life of the party? Do you want to challenge your friends to be better people? The way you want to represent yourself in the world has everything to do with how you communicate.

## How Evolved Grown Ups Interact

Dynamic communicators convey specifically what they need and want instead of speaking in generalities that may be misinterpreted. They don't expect that others will read their minds and know what they want. They do more than complain; they offer solutions. If they don't have solutions, they ask for help and listen to advice. Dynamic communicators always try for a compromise, because they want all parties to walk away satisfied. They do not tell others what they should or should not do. They do not impose their own thoughts, wishes, and values onto others in an aggressive way, though they may point out things in a constructive manner.

Dynamic communicators don't bring up twenty things that happened in the past—with anyone. They are focused on the here and now and the future and moving forward. A dynamic communicator clears her head of the chattering voices and thinks clearly about how she feels and what she wants before venturing forth to have an important conversation.

Dynamic communicators find intelligent ways to ask for things instead of cursing, screaming, or threatening. They don't dump things on people or project onto new people events that have happened in their pasts. They don't accuse others of cheating, lying, or stealing based on what might have happened in the past. Dynamic interaction is dependent on your ability to recognize that you are affected by your unique past and issues but can still engage confidently in the here-and-now conversation.

A person who has been cheated on or lied to in a former relationship may freak out when the new person she is dating shows up two hours late one night. Because of her baggage, her mind races through all the worst scenarios and assumes that her date is with somebody else. Dynamic communicators do not succumb to these irrational thoughts; they deal in facts. They don't confront; they gather information.

A dynamic communicator knows when the time has come for that long-overdue talk or when to walk away and cut communications altogether or what tool to employ along the way so it doesn't come to either of those extremes. If you don't know what the tool is, you can certainly say, "I need to think about this." Then talk to friends, reflect, get advice, and then get back to the person you want to speak with. The more toxic the relationship is, the more you'll have to take care to do that. If, for example, your mother is difficult and one day says something particularly rude, you might say, "Mom I have to run, let me get back to you." Stop, breathe, and take the time to decide what to say when you next speak to her.

A dynamic communicator has good impulse control. You have to be able to control your impulse to scream back at a yeller, to bulldoze somebody into doing what you want, to withdraw and walk away. Whatever form of poor communication you're dealing with, resist the temptation to sink to its level. Little kids and teenagers have poor impulse control. So do many people who have had traumatic childhoods, people with control issues who need anger management, and addicts. If you are always going on the attack regardless of the reason, or stomping away, you will never be a dynamic interacter—or a true grown up.

The whole goal is to walk away from unpleasant people and difficult situations feeling all right—not necessarily great, but not devastated. That comes from realizing that the person you are dealing with has not mastered dynamic interaction and that you sometimes have to let it go, for your own peace of mind if nothing else. Be the best communicator you can be; set the right example, hope for the best, and carry on.

## Taking on Technology

The past ten years have brought miraculous advances to the way we all communicate. With BlackBerrys, texting, IMing, and cell phones, none of us ever needs to be out of touch again. The whole world has changed: I can be at lunch with a friend, on the beach with my child, or in a business meeting and still communicate with somebody. I can be lost on the road and get directions with a punch of a button. I can work away from the office. And though all these innovations are meant to help us communicate better and faster, this technology brings with it a new and daunting set of obstacles.

The problem is twofold: some people become so addicted to certain forms of communication that they no longer engage in heart-to-heart, face-to-face communication. Fully capable grown ups face difficult situations head-on. They can have that uncomfortable discussion with a friend when they're angry, not just send an e-mail. They can break up with someone in person or at least over the phone, not just send a text or change the person's Facebook status. Many people are now relying on technology to either make requests that they find uncomfortable to do in person or to tell someone off. Technology is allowing people to avoid upsetting situations and any possible confrontations, changing social norms that have existed since the beginning of time.

The other problem is the false sense of intimacy that comes from a highly technological relationship. There's no real intimacy there, and e-mail and texts are prone to misinterpretation. I sent an e-mail to someone the other day, and she thought I was kidding. I didn't put a smiley face or ha-ha there, but I realized when she and I actually came face-to-face that what I thought was perfectly appropriate, clear communication had been badly misinterpreted. There's a whole lot less misinterpretation when people get together in person. Nonverbal cues often give us as much information about what someone is saying as her chosen words. If this woman had been sitting in front of me when I delivered my exact words, she would have seen that I wasn't laughing. We could have nipped that problem right in the bud.

It's becoming a common complaint that technology is actually keeping couples apart; it's letting people think, *Well, I've communicated with you by e-mail or text message today, so I can come home and read my book or watch TV because we've already connected.* Relationships thrive on intimacy, and true intimacy includes face-to-face discussions, spending time together in shared activities, and physical contact. In terms of dating or marriage, use technology to enhance your relationship, not take it over.

**How you communicate sets the tone for how the world sees you** and treats you. Dynamic communicators get along much easier and better in the world. It's that old example: be great to your waitress and you might get a free dessert. Be horrible and demanding and rude and she might spit into your food. How you communicate has everything to do with what you get back out of life. Our goal in this book is for you to get more of everything you want!

**3**

# Deal
# or No Deal

**C**hildhood is a time of powerlessness, a proverbial card game where, from the moment you are born, you are forced to play with the cards you were dealt. Your hand of life includes your genetic cards that predispose much about your health, appearance, and personality. You are also dealt cards that determine your life circumstances. You have no say in what kind of house, apartment, or neighborhood you are raised in, whether or not you have siblings, what your parents do and how they act, who takes care of you, the school you attend, whether you are rich or poor, or even if you're allowed to eat dinner in front of the television!

Do you ever look back and remember feeling like your life as a child just happened to you? Maybe your best friend moved away, your father lost his job, your mother drank too much, you had a wonderful first-grade teacher, or your grandmother baked the best chocolate-chip cookies. Perhaps your parents or caregivers yelled all the time or worked all the time or struggled to make ends meet. Maybe you had many friends, or a few friends, or even a kid in school who was mean to you. All of these life circumstances, both the good and the bad, were out of your control—and so began your need to learn to cope.

Every person's ability to cope begins in childhood, but how you behave in adulthood is a combination of the cards you were dealt as a child, your life experiences as you've grown, and the baggage you have accumulated along the way.

So, you were dealt a hand at birth, had some hurtful experiences and some great times, and accumulated some baggage along the way. Now you are an adult. Your life has been shaped by those past experiences, and they continue to affect the choices you make now that you have far more power and control. To stick with our metaphor, picture an all-night card game: sometimes you're winning, with a huge pile of chips, and other times you lose your money in ten minutes flat. Those results come from the cards you were dealt and the choices you made while playing the game—and your life works exactly the same way.

I like the card-game analogy because many of the cards, good and bad, you are dealt come from the luck of the draw. Some people were blessed with happy, secure upbringings and seem to get all the breaks from that point on, all the time. You might ask yourself: *Why them? Why can't things come easy like that for me?* The fact that some of us just have to work harder at life seems unfair. Add to it that we less lucky ones need to have superior coping skills to be successful. That said, the reality is that no one has it all, no one escapes life unscathed, and the downside for people who seem so lucky is that they can be poorly equipped to handle difficulties; after all, they've become so accustomed to having life go their way.

I have a bit of good news for you. No matter what kind of hand you are holding, the fantastic benefit of being a grown up is that you get to trade in those cards. Yes! It's true, once you embrace the skills of being a grown up and plan the hand you want to create, you can begin trading in the cards that were forced upon you for the cards of your choice! What kind of relationship do you want to have with your parents—or do you even want one at all? Do you want to live in the same town, state, or even country that you grew up in? Up the street from family, or a continent away? Do you want to live in a city, or on a farm? Do you want to get married? Do you want to raise a family, or not have children? All of a sudden, you get to add all the cards you like to your hand. Don't let fear or defeats from your past trap you in the mindset of, *I hate the cards I was dealt . . . I got a bad deal . . . This game is rigged . . . I can't cope . . .*; if you do, you'll never seek new cards, and you'll never be happy with your deal.

In recent years a number of research studies about aging and end-of-life satisfaction have been conducted. What we've learned is that the men and women who look back on their lives and conclude, "I worked hard toward accomplishing everything I wanted and achieved many of my goals," are the people who grow old peacefully and with few regrets. The lesson for us all to take to heart now is that all the time and energy you expend bemoaning the bad hand you've been dealt is wasted time and energy. Instead, focus on what you can change now, and begin to invest your efforts in those directions.

How you play out your hand is a matter of motivation, training, and skill. All those dissatisfied, overwhelmed, stressed-to-the-max men and women out there with far too much on their plates—and that's many people I know—could improve their lives immeasurably by learning more effective coping skills and then putting them into practice. In this chapter I'm going to teach you the tools that will allow you to better handle whatever life throws at you from this point forward. The goal is to manage your life with much greater ease and enjoyment. To walk away from the game of life feeling like a winner!

## Coping Models

The people who first care for us in our lives are the role models who show us how to cope. The learning process starts instinctively and is based on how the first caregivers in our lives respond to us. When we won't stop crying, are they tense or relaxed? When we scream and yell, do they comfort us, reason with us, or yell back or spank us? When a baby is crying, the phone's ringing, the doorbell is buzzing, and the pot on the stove is boiling over, how does Mom or Dad handle it? We register their feelings and reactions to these moments well before we are consciously aware of them and way before we can articulate them. Parents transmit their anxiety, anger, or calm to us, so we learn early on that that's the way to respond to turmoil or pressure.

If you have parents who take a deep breath and can handle chaos all around them well, they are providing you an excellent first role model on how to cope. The opposite, of course, is also true. When my daughter was young, I hired a woman to watch her two days a week while I went to work. She was nurturing and kind but had a tremendous fear of germs from the park. She used to bring a towel with her and lay it down on the slide before my daughter slid down, making sliding difficult. She placed a towel over the swing before placing my daughter in it. I started to notice that when I took my daughter to the park myself, she would get hysterical if I did not have a towel with me to put down on the equipment. She would get agitated, cry, and become anxious. She had "learned" that all the equipment at the park was dirty and not to be touched, ever, without a towel. All of this before she could speak! My daughter had learned to cope at the park only under specific conditions. Here, with a babysitter who was around her only a minimal amount of time, the smallest of influences had a tremendous impact on my daughter's coping skills. Needless to say, I put a stop to the towel business.

Parents not only transmit their own emotional reactions to stressors, but must choose how much attention and work they are willing to do when they see how their child responds to stress. For example, the child's responses will soon become ingrained if parents do not step in. If parents provide an appropriate amount of reassurance and tell a child, "You're fine," then a dropped ice-cream cone or fall on the playground does not become a scene. That child learns to begin to tell himself that he will survive this crisis. The child will build his inner confidence level so that he feels generally able to cope with whatever situation arises.

The ways in which our parents and caregivers teach us to cope and handle stress are quickly absorbed. We all have tapes that play in our minds, which were created over time from a very young age. These tapes come from all the people who were around us and tended to say certain phrases or reacted in consistent ways over and over again, until these messages were implanted in our brains. When stress hits, the tapes start to roll: *you'll be fine; you can handle this; I know it's scary, but you can manage . . .* or *I can't deal with this . . . it's too much for me to handle . . . I'm going to lose my mind.*

Every elementary school has a standard set of procedures and drills in place to handle emergency situations such as fires, earthquakes, and hurricanes. They drill the kids over and over in maneuvers like stop, drop, and roll; or crawl under your desk; or get in line and leave the building slowly. The class practices these maneuvers over and over until they become second nature and the kids respond automatically. This is the beginning of instilling coping skills in kids for panicky situations at school, but it also can set the tone for how we develop as grown ups. Ideally, you have a parent who has operated in much the same way, teaching you calm, methodical drills—tools and procedures that will help you overcome a scary situation and begin to teach you how to cope.

Tapes are different from the voices we spoke about in the previous chapter. Our voices run the tapes! The tapes in our minds are repetitive statements that we've heard over and over throughout the course of our lives that immediately start to play when a stressful situation arises. If you had a mother who was high strung and a father who was laid back, you will likely play a tape that reflects one of those two attitudes. Sometimes, two tapes from opposing viewpoints start to roll and compete in your mind, which could paralyze you into not coping in any way at all, healthy or not. Consistency is tremendously important, which is why it is so essential for parents and caregivers to at least attempt to get on the same page in terms of their responses.

The reality is that few people are raised by someone who consistently copes in an optimum manner. The challenge we face as adults is functioning in a healthy way despite how we were impacted by the varying coping skills of our caregivers. See if you recognize your own upbringing or parenting style in any of these behaviors from the five basic types of role models for coping—I certainly see them all the time!

## The Helicopter Caregiver

This hypervigilant parent is constantly in your face, keeping his eyes on you, always. He won't even let you drop a cup—he's right there to catch it. This person will handle every problem that arises; if you don't like what you're wearing or spill on your favorite outfit or hate your dinner, he runs to get another shirt, tissue, or alternate meal. There is a tremendous sense of security and safety that comes with this sort of caregiving. The problem with this style is that you never have to learn coping skills, because all of your needs are met. You begin to expect that someone will always be there to handle tough situations for you. The other downside is that at some point people who are raised like this may feel smothered, start to rebel, and want to break loose and fend for themselves.

I recently ran into a client while we were both waiting with our children at the doctor's office. My client's five-year-old daughter was clutching a tattered teddy bear. Trying to make conversation, I looked at the little girl and said, "What is your bear's name?" "Teddy," answered her mother. The next thing I knew, my entire line of questioning that I was directing toward the daughter was answered by the mother. She wouldn't let her kid get a word in edgewise.

We have some family friends whose sons, age nine and eleven, love to eat hamburgers with no bun. We went out to dinner with them one night, and the sons ordered their usual. When the food arrived, their father jumped up to cut their meat into bite-size pieces (like you would for a two- or three-year-old). I couldn't help myself and whispered quietly to their mother, "How come you don't have them cut the meat themselves? They are old enough; don't they get embarrassed?" Her answer: "My husband wants to keep them young; we never let them use a knife." Both of these examples involve kindhearted, well-meaning parents who are hovering dangerously near the point of preventing their children from learning not only communication skills when meeting a new person, but the bigger picture of developing independence and a mastery of basic coping skills (like feeding yourself!).

If you were raised with a hovering parent, you might seek a hovering spouse—someone who handles the responsibility of the finances, earning a living, discipline of children, and the family social calendar. You become attached to someone who will take care of and handle all your problems, so you don't have to cope. Or, you may go the other way and become a hoverer yourself and seek out someone passive whose life you can manage.

## The Clueless Caregiver

This parent is so distracted by his or her own troubles, addictions, or problems that he or she barely notices if the house is on fire, let alone how a child is coping with a spilled drink. Their attention, for whatever reason, is impossible to get. The plus side to this kind of caregiver is that you may enjoy a great deal of freedom, which can force you to learn to take care of yourself and handle many situations yourself. The downside is that you are missing having a solid parental role model, you are forced to parent yourself, and you will certainly suffer more injuries, more conflict, and more chaos in your life when there are no grown ups keeping a watchful eye out.

I once knew a very mischievous little boy. His parents were well aware of this tendency too! One day, Mom and Dad were in the family room, watching television, when little three-and-a-half-year-old Kevin came walking into the room. They barely looked up as their son grabbed a footstool and walked out. Over the course of the next five minutes Kevin returned to the family room five more times. He took the yellow pages, a pillow, a large decorative wooden box, a crate, and a large stack of manila envelopes. Now, I have to ask: would you have been curious about what he might be up to at this point? I sure was, but they were hardly paying attention.

All of a sudden they heard a squeaking and crackling noise and their son's happy squealing from the dining room. They ran in to find little Kevin had piled up the phone book, pillow, stool, box, crate, and envelopes on top of the dining room table and was swinging from the chandelier! The squeaking and crackling noise was the drywall in the ceiling breaking from the weight and movement of this activity! How would they have coped with a huge injury had the ceiling collapsed?

Another parent I knew was busy getting ready for work and told her five-year-old son to grab something for show-and-tell at school. Because they were late and rushing, she put him in the car hurriedly, talked on her cell phone during the entire car ride, and dropped him off at school with barely a break in her conversation. Around ten o'clock her cell phone rang. Her son's teacher informed her that he was being suspended for two days. He had taken the three-foot genuine spear off the wall in his father's office and brought it to school for show-and-tell. Though he had carried it out the door and into the car and then into school, Mom never even noticed it in his hand. How will this boy cope if he continues to get suspended or, worse, thrown out of school for bad behavior?

Many times kids who are raised by an oblivious parent have no sense of appropriate boundaries or urgency. This is the adult who can't be bothered to be on time for a big meeting and wonders why everyone doesn't just understand. They have trouble managing daily challenges, their lives just lurch along, but they aren't worried about it.

## The Laid-Back Caregiver

This parent is completely unruffled by anything. Oh, she'll notice when you fall down or are upset about something, but she takes it all in stride. "Oh, it could be a broken arm. Let's get in the car and go see the doctor." "Oh, you ate seven bowls of ice cream at that party, you're going to feel sick tonight; we'll just put a bucket by your bed." The plus side of this is that clearly, this parent doesn't suffer from anxiety or is in denial about it, which makes it much less likely that she'll raise anxious children. They will likely grow up to become laid-back, easygoing people themselves. The downside can be a lack of limits and boundaries. This person with the laid-back role model might eat ice cream and Fritos for dinner all of his life because he always has. He'll also tend to not be great at picking up warning signs of dangerous situations or people.

On Saturday and Sunday mornings the Smith children make their own breakfast while Mom and Dad sleep in. The rules are that they can make anything that is "breakfast appropriate" and they need to clean up. Last week, the boys ate a quarter of the specially decorated sheet cake that had been bought for their uncle's birthday party that evening. The parents weren't thrilled, but they ended up picking up a pound cake and strawberries (it was the easiest) on the way to the party. Despite the relatives' being disappointed, as was Uncle Joe, the Smith parents said, "Oh, well, it was just a cake. Joe will have another birthday next year." Their kids are not learning to face other people's emotions. How will they cope if someone actually becomes alienated because they have no concern for others?

One day I ventured into a fast-food restaurant with a children's play area. Mom and Dad were reading the morning paper while their kids were running around flinging pickles from their burgers onto the paintings on the wall, trying to see if they would stick. The manager came over, reprimanded the entire family, and told them they were never allowed back. Dad's response? He whispered to the kids, "He won't remember us if we come back in a few weeks." How will these kids cope when there are real consequences for their bad behaviors?

Laid-back caregivers are far from the worst option—men and women raised this way often walk around saying, "It's all fine, I'm okay," and they believe it. Not too much shakes them. The problems arise when things aren't all right; these adults have trouble recognizing when there really is a problem. They tend to think they're handling everything just fine, everything will work out in the end, and they don't worry enough about it.

## The Drill Sergeant Caregiver

This caregiver is screaming, yelling, and criticizing the minute your ball runs into the street or you strike out when playing T-ball. He tends to be very invested in demanding respect and refuses to raise a whiny, needy child. This is the kind of parent who tosses his kid off a dock and says, "Sink or swim." Life itself with this kind of parent is basically sink or swim—he is toughening you up and forcing you to learn to cope—for your own good. This may cause some kids to shut down and have no coping skills at all out of fear; they grow up to become timid, risk-averse adults. A child raised in this type of environment is often unable to take in information from other people at all; she is so afraid of what she's going to get from the drill sergeant that other, more reasonable voices are ignored.

I know a family where the kids iron their clothes every morning, do an hour of calisthenics each day, and are not allowed to socialize with families whose children don't dress by their father's strict standards. The kids have a great work ethic in school but have trouble making friends—they have each been allowed only one at this present time, as the others at their school have been deemed "unacceptable."

Ricky played Little League baseball for two years until his verbally abusive father yelled at him so much about his playing that he quit. The same thing happened with basketball, football, and track. Ricky's father was so offensive that he was kicked off the fields and courts at least once each and every season. Ricky eventually quit sports altogether and retreated into a world of alcohol and drugs. I met him when he was thirteen and had recently attempted suicide. Ricky had been beaten down so far that he couldn't cope anymore, and the only solution he could see was to take his own life. Thankfully, this life-and-death crisis finally spurred his mother to leave his father, and now Ricky and his mom are trying to rebuild their lives.

The upside of this kind of parent is that these children are generally forced into a strict routine, which isn't necessarily bad in and of itself. They definitely learn discipline—another good trait. Their coping skills are very regimented. However, the downside is that an adult who was raised by a drill sergeant is often fearful and anxious and lets others walk all over her, though she carries an underlying anger. She has quite a temper under her mild exterior because she was helpless to rage back at her parent. Other children of drill sergeants emulate the caregiver and become real hotheads, taking every opportunity to scream at and bully others.

## The True Grown-Up Caregiver

This parent has elements of all of the above caregiving styles but knows how to respond to pressure appropriately. She takes things as they come—objectively. A real grown up can rise to the occasion when she needs to respond and react at maximum capacity and relax when it's better to let the small stuff go.

Karen's children typically get straight A's, but this past year her daughter started getting wrapped up in her friends, her grades began to drop, and she was ditching school all the time. Karen didn't know how to handle her daughter or even how to cope with such a situation, as they had never had issues before. Karen talked with her friends and family to see if they had any ideas. Karen was referred to a Toughlove parenting program in her area that offered her the tools and support to come up with a solid plan to get her daughter back on track. This included no time with friends until the grades came up again and mandatory attendance at school or she would not get a car at age sixteen. Her daughter was angry but wanted her social life back and especially her future car. She pushed herself to study hard, got her grades back up, and attended class every day. In turn, she got her friend privileges back and is now happily looking at cars.

Kimmy is eight years old and very picky about what she eats. So particular that she often refuses food at other people's houses because they have nothing in their kitchen that she will eat. Her parents initially tried to accommodate her every whim, preparing special meals, sending to-go meals to other houses, and avoiding serving foods that she didn't like. They were running their lives and their meals around her! I let them know that Kimmy needed to learn to cope, that they should have foods in the house that she would eat, but that they also needed to set boundaries around how far they were willing to go. They were so busy enabling her that it was making her even more picky! After a month of rigidly following the new plan, they are all less stressed, and Kimmy has learned that she must cope by finding something acceptable to eat if she is hungry or choosing to not eat at all.

**Everybody moves in and out of these personas all the time. We're** not looking at the ideal superparent or caregiver; everybody falls into some of these behaviors we discussed above at one point or another.

It's just a question of balance. Real grown ups respond to a fire like it's a fire and a skinned knee like it's a skinned knee. They see things for what they are, they are mindful, they have planned ahead, they give children enough room to figure things out on their own while offering guidance and support when needed. How many people grow up with a calm, stabilizing force to help them when they are melting down? Not many. Those who do have a great head start on becoming real grown ups in terms of their coping skills, because they were guided into successfully coping for themselves. For those who didn't have a great role model, it's a matter of identifying potentially destructive coping mechanisms and consciously replacing them with healthier behaviors until they become integrated into who you are.

## Crisis Management

On a normal, regular day there are plenty of minor annoyances to contend with. These might include traffic jams, other people running late, the babysitter not showing up, the dog or child messing up the carpet, or the grocery store not having what you need. For the sake of our health and peace of mind, it behooves us all to learn to react calmly and refuse to lose control over what are essentially unavoidable minor problems. Real grown ups realize that in the grand scheme of life, they will live, their jobs or careers will go on, and they will still be able to function. They will handle it with ease when there is dog vomit on the carpet when neighbors unexpectedly come over. They realize when they are getting a little overheated, they take a deep breath, and they know they're going to be okay. Oh, sure, they get mad or stressed out for a minute, but then they move on.

A truly major crisis—terminal illness, death, divorce, financial ruin, loss of a job—can bring even the master coper to her knees.

These are the big life challenges that face everyone sooner or later. One of the best tools for dealing with a major crisis is to lean on your support system, which we'll discuss in detail in the next chapter. Here's how your support system comes into play in terms of coping. My theory is that the more major the crisis, the more people you should share your experience and feelings with. There is comfort and calm to be gained from exchanging information and feeling free to express what's happening and telling your story. The more people you tell about your challenge, the better, simply to get different viewpoints and take advantage of a wide variety of people's different skills and knowledge.

Even if those you lean on don't have the answer, they will be calmer and more objective about whatever is happening in your life. A friend can be calm, rational, and reasonable when your emotions are running high. Two friends are even better—few people are willing to hear you complain all the time. The important note here is that we all need to hear the voice of reason during a difficult time. If what you're hearing in your own mind isn't helpful or you feel incapable of even having a logical thought, then it's important to reach out to someone who can help you manage what you're going through. If you know you are incapable, then all you need to know is that you need to go find someone, or several someones, who can help.

I urge you to tell your story to as many people as you possibly can. The release will make you feel better, and many will want to reach out and help. You will get guidance that you can't get by suffering alone and in silence. It's more than just telling everybody; it's talking to key people and figuring out who can help you with this particular crisis you are enduring. It's about finding the right person to network with to help you find a job, if that's the problem. If there's a death in the family, who can you count on to make funeral arrangements, accompany you to the service, help with the finances?

If the crisis is an illness, who do you know who knows good doctors? If it's a divorce, who knows a good attorney or can fix you up on a date? Grown ups know that leveraging your support system—getting others to help you find who to go to for help—is the key to coping with and managing these situations.

During a major crisis most people's minds are racing so fast that they go into automatic panic and fear overdrive. I recommend that people facing a terrible problem sit down at the earliest possible moment, breathe, and make a list: what needs to get done immediately, what can be put aside, and who can help at each step. A real grown up tries all along to be forward thinking. If he knows the economy is bad, or if his situation at work is tenuous, he looks ahead and prepares for that. A real grown up does not stick his head in the sand. He prepares for crisis in the future!

It is not my expectation that, real grown up or not, anyone should be able to deal with every crisis appropriately at all times. When tragedy befalls, anyone will fall apart. No matter how many tools you have in place to function—everything that has worked before in your life—you probably don't have the tools for this current tragedy; nor should you. These are uncharted waters. Again, this is where your support system comes in. A person who is a real grown up will certainly fall apart under certain circumstances. But she does eventually realize that she cannot handle it, she cannot cope, and so she sets out to find people to tell her what she does not know.

## The Elevator Effect

A common coping problem to become aware of and avoid is what I call the elevator effect, which means escalating a problem to a higher level than it is. This is when you go to the doctor and he informs you that something doesn't look right in one of your tests. The elevator effect causes you to go home and start planning your funeral. Or let's say you are told that there may be some budget cuts in your job, and you go home and say to your spouse, "We're going to be homeless. We'd better move in with your parents!" Being prepared means gathering information and facts. It's about seeing more doctors, asking your boss for more specifics—getting all the information you can so you can freak out at the appropriate level!

"My boyfriend broke up with me. I'm going to be alone forever." We all have those doomsday moments, when we think that way: "I'll never find someone to love; I'm going to wind up homeless," "I'm going to die," or, "I'm going to kill someone." A true grown up has these thoughts occasionally but doesn't act on them! It's perfectly normal.

I was once speaking to a police officer about a woman who had threatened to kill her husband. "Everybody wants to kill their husband or wife at one point or another," he told me. "The people who start making a plan are the ones we worry about. I gather all the information I can before we start making arrests and hauling people into the station."

## Optimum Coping

Grown ups who know how to play the cards they're dealt are happier, less stressed, and more desirable friends, partners, employees, and bosses. Mastering the following skills will make your life a whole lot easier and ensure you will be a much more pleasant person to be around:

Managing your own anxiety

Being as prepared as possible to handle a crisis

Relinquishing control and remaining as unaffected as possible by minor problems

Having the ability to reach out to someone who can help when you don't know what to do

Refusing to stick your head in the sand; gathering information to assess the reality of the situation

Weighing the options and responding the best way you can at the time

Recognizing a challenge for what it is without succumbing to the elevator effect

Conserving energy for real emergencies

Taking some sort of action. Yes, everyone is entitled to a day or three in bed, sulking, or a drunken night out, sobbing, or a food binge. But after that, a real grown up takes some sort of action. Taking action doesn't necessarily mean solving the problem at hand; the problem might be too big. It means doing something proactive to get yourself out of the rut you're in.

I understand that those who had an abusive childhood, grew up in poverty, were shuffled around all the time, lived through deaths or other family tragedies at a young age—anyone who struggled with a great burden early on—may be unlikely to just pick up and start coping in an ideal way. Even those who had pretty "normal" childhoods carry scars and burdens. Those who fall into this category may need to seek counseling to heal the wounds of the past, so they can learn to deal with whatever else is dealt to them in the future in a constructive way.

Take a look at the cards you're dealing with right now, and ask yourself if you're happy with them. The cards that you're happy with, keep. The ones you are not happy about, start figuring out how to turn them in. Life is an ongoing opportunity to draw new cards. Maybe you didn't want to change your cards one bit, but you were forced to. Resolve to choose a more positive way to respond to upheaval! Look at it as a great opportunity to stop any dysfunctional behavior and start behaving like a grown up!

# I Get By
# with a Little Help
# from My Friends

**W**hen you were a child, who was your best friend? Was it your next-door neighbor? A classmate from school? How did you meet? Why were you two so close? How much time did you spend together? What kinds of activities did you enjoy? I would guess that at such a young age you weren't consciously aware of seeking out any specific traits in your friend; it didn't matter if she was tall or short, fast or slow, rich or poor. It didn't matter how you met, what kind of house she lived in, or what her family background was like. That person was your special friend because she filled your days with fun and companionship.

Chances are good that the reason this friend I've got you thinking about became your best friend was because of her proximity to you. That means you two had easy access to each other on a regular basis. Maybe your closest companion was a family member—a brother, sister, or cousin, especially if you were close in age—for this very reason. Perhaps your friend's parents and yours were friends and they lived around the corner from you, or you and your friend were in classes or activities together. You likely had similar interests—whether that was playing Barbie, building forts, or watching TV together—but ultimately what created your bond was simply the ease of your ability to spend time together. I see this over and over once kids start school. They tend to become closest to the children in their classrooms. Classmates eat lunch together, hang out on the playground, and choose each other for teams at school. Friendships and "best friends" often fluctuate each year as classrooms are reassigned and kids are thrown into contact with a new group.

Only a few short years earlier in their lives, as infants and toddlers, children didn't "need" friends. Babies put into a room with other infants during the first two years of life engage in what child development experts call "parallel play"; they barely interact and might even ignore the other children even if they are playing right next to one another. They lack the desire, skills, and tools to connect and become friends. As children grow older, interaction with one another begins and is often anything but peaceful. Having the chance to peek into a playdate with a couple of two-year-olds, we might see them both grabbing for the same toy and shouting "Me! Mine, mine, mine!" The need for ownership of the toy far outweighs the desire for companionship and interaction.

It is just around this time in a toddler's life that parents, teachers, and caregivers step in to help educate children on how to enjoy the toy together so the child not only has that special toy but the benefit of a playmate too. "Now, let's take turns with that ball," or "Maybe we should find a game that you *can* play together." Parents, schools, and children's programs work hard to help children learn to interact, support one another, and work toward common goals as a team. You might hear teachers say, "Billy, why don't you go help Jimmy build that house with blocks?" or, "Sara, why don't you and Debbie take turns on that bicycle?" Our parents ideally are taking a similar attitude at home as well, saying things like, "Play nicely with your sister," "Please take your little brother to the bathroom for me," or, "The Scotts are coming over this afternoon, so please be nice to their son Jimmy—they are our guests."

All of these cues are about stimulating give-and-take and the building of relationships. When we look at the continued development of friendships and a support network, we must talk about the teen years. Developmentally speaking, this is the time when we begin to truly separate from our parents, become our own persons, and turn to our peer group for a higher level of support and connection. As a young child, no doubt you wanted to sit by your parents, ride in *their* car, and hold *their* hands. As a teen, you wanted your parents sitting somewhere else, you wanted to drive your *own* car, and would have died of embarrassment if your mom or dad tried to hold your hand in public *or* in private! It doesn't matter if you were the head cheerleader in high school or held the school record for talking too much; whether you were in the band, a total academic, or the big jock—you began to turn outward to interact and bond with a peer group outside of your family.

You sought advice, support, and encouragement from your friends. If you didn't know what to wear, you asked them. If you had a crush on someone, you told them. If you had gossip to share, they heard it first. These intense adolescent relationships and experiences set the tone for how our support needs evolve, and build on the foundation that was set for us as young children.

As a child . . .

Were you outgoing, or shy?

How big was your circle of friends?

Were you happy alone and needed to be coaxed to play with others?

Did you approach new social situations with confidence, or dread them?

How did your parents help or hurt you in these situations?

As an adolescent . . .

Were you a bully, or were you bullied?

Were you a leader, or a follower?

Did you have a big group of friends, or stick close to one best friend?

Were you chatty, or shy?

Were you a joiner involved in lots of activities, or a loner?

Were you passive, or aggressive?

These questions are food for thought as you consider your support system today. Looking back and assessing your early social experiences is helpful because knowing who you were back then will help you better understand who you are now and where you'd like to go from here.

Ultimately, our early life friendship and relationship lessons lay the groundwork for all of us to build the support systems we will need to navigate the waters of our grown-up lives. And let's be honest: getting along and playing nicely with others is in our own best interest! If nothing else, some of our friends have "toys" we don't have—and more important, we have come to realize that having someone to play with, talk to, and confide in is fun and one of life's greatest joys.

## The Four-Step System

Certainly we all know some adults who are all about "Me! Mine, mine, mine!" You know—that self-centered, narcissistic person who sounds and often acts like a two-year-old but has the face of an adult? There are quite a few of them out there—hopefully you haven't allowed too many of them to be in your world. But don't worry, if you have, we will address that later in this chapter. Either way, the good news is that if you're reading this book, you are growth-oriented, care about both yourself and others, and have thus learned over the years to appreciate the benefits that a friend, colleague, or companion offers you in terms of stimulation, conversation, and entertainment. If you value these things, then you're on the right track already, but my concept of building a quality and successful support system goes well beyond that.

A fully loaded, Stacy Kaiser–recommended support system provides fun and social interaction, encouragement, support, and help during tough times, cheerleaders to root for you during your challenges, and people who will celebrate your victories. Not to mention go-to sources for assistance and advice on everything from how to program your computer to recommending a good doctor, to driving your child home from school when you're stuck in a meeting, to bringing you chicken soup when you can't get out of bed. This support system is designed to meet the needs you have that you can't meet yourself. It's a soft place to land, and it's the area where you most want to give back. A high-functioning grown up has a solid system in place, and our goal here is to show you how to assess and build your own.

For the moment, I would like to believe that your reading this book means you have allowed me to be part of your support system—you are letting me into your world by seeking help and new tools to better your life. Now that you have reached out and brought me into your circle, let me guide you into growing and improving your support system so you can get the maximum benefits from the people around you and their resources. As you have likely already discovered, because I've mentioned it many times already, it is my belief that the power to change your life comes first with focusing on *you*. Yes, even though this chapter is about other people, those others are chosen by you, needed by you, and catered to by you. Hence, the common denominator is—*you*! So, let's assess *who you are and what you need*.

Think about it, and please be honest with yourself as we work toward maximizing the relationships in your life: Are you somebody who tends to be on the needy side? In your relationships, do you demand that the other person always be readily and instantly available? Whenever you call, do you *need* her to answer the phone? Should she drop everything for you? Or are you somebody who is more independent and can go for long periods of time without seeing or talking with the people in your circle, just as long as you know they're there? Do you need versatile friends—those who could just as easily accompany you to a work function or a baseball game or a party? Are you a "friend compartmentalizer"—someone who has your sports friend, your cocktail-party friend, your work friend, and your advice friend? Are you somebody who prides herself on self-reliance and is reluctant to ask anybody for help? Are you the one all your friends turn to in an emergency? Or are you somebody who needs constant help, shoring up, and reassurance? Your answers to these questions should help you begin to think about the kinds of friends and support you need.

Some men and women are hardwired as very outgoing creatures. Many become what I call friend collectors—they are social and find the greatest pleasure in life meeting and collecting new friends and acquaintances, just as others collect books or figurines. Others, particularly those who are by nature shyer, prefer more intimate relationships, or maybe just one with one good friend. There's an easy way to figure out which kind of person you are and what you need: examine your support system history. Look back on all the friends and supportive relationships you've had throughout your life and the people who have been there for you or have not; have you been satisfied? Have they provided enough of what you need? Have they been there enough? These are the questions I tell people to ask themselves as they evaluate their current support system as well.

If you've generally been satisfied with the help and feedback and support you get from your one friend or twenty, then your support system is working for you. If you haven't been satisfied, and you've been longing for something more, it's important to stop and take a good hard look at what it is you're doing—or not doing—that is impacting your ability to create a solid support network.

Here are the main questions to ponder when it comes to evaluating the support in your life:

> Who do I have, how do they help me, and is what they offer enough?

> If I fall, who will pick me up?

I know a number of people who complain on a regular basis that they don't have a good support system. They don't feel part of anything, they don't feel like they have any close friends, and yet they stay home every night watching television or reading a book—alone. Those people do not have a solid support system for a good reason: they are not putting themselves out there and doing the work to build one! That's what people need to realize: you have to put out the effort to get the rewards.

In high school and college, a huge pool of potential friends, all around the same age and with roughly the same interests, is easily accessible to you. Additionally, schools typically have built-in resources for support in the form of libraries, guidance counselors, career advisors, and activity- and social-interest-based clubs. The combination of these things helps provide an excellent support system for anyone who is interested in taking advantage of them. As we get older, many adults fall into a rut and discover that the potential to meet new friends and build a support network dwindles drastically. They get busy with their day-to-day lives. They wake up, go to work with the same people every day, return home, eat, and spend time with their significant other or family. This can leave even the most outgoing and open person feeling isolated and without a sense of community.

However, and this is the good news: the advantage to being a grown up is that if you put in the effort and reach out to connect with others, you benefit from the freedom of choice—*you* get to chose who you interact with, who you lean on, who you want to give back to, and who becomes a part of your support network. As a child, your relationships are circumscribed by what your parents allow you access to. If your best friends move away and your parents aren't willing to drive you to visit them, or if they forbid you from spending time with certain persons—then you can't see them. As an adult, you can initiate and keep up relationships with whomever you please.

So, here you are an adult. You have the freedom to spend time with and invest in whomever you chose. You now realize the value of support and a sense of community, and you are ready to take action. How do you do it? You follow my four-step process to maximize your support system: FIND, CULTIVATE, MAINTAIN, and EVALUATE.

FIND people—at a class, at work, online, through introductions, standing in line, in your office building . . . the list is endless. For those who complain there's no one to meet, there are a whole lot of people in the world you don't know, and some of them would like to be your friend. One idea I love is to try something new once a month: a new dog park, a different class, a restaurant in a new neighborhood. Go somewhere you've never been before to meet new people.

This is the first and most important step—finding people. And to find people, seek out new activities if your routine keeps you from seeing many new faces. You need to work on building your support system as if it were your part-time job—whether that means getting involved in community activities, volunteering, taking a class two nights a month, or going to the gym three times a week.

A word to those whose shyness prevents them from connecting with new people: I myself used to be shy, and after I graduated from college, I used to attend cocktail parties and work functions that were full of people I didn't know. I never said a word, because I had no idea what to talk about. No one would have mistaken me for any kind of good communicator. Because I didn't talk, people immediately assumed I was unfriendly or stuck up. When you're a blank slate, people will project their own opinions onto you.

I eventually came up with the idea to be ready to talk about five current events every time I had to go to a function—whether that was the weather, the top local political story, some gossip about a celebrity—and would have those conversation pieces ready depending on who I spoke to. It was important to me that I wasn't perceived as a wallflower. Twenty years later I still talk about my conversation piece of the day! It has become second nature, and I'm not introverted at parties anymore.

The huge upside to the Internet and modern technology is that nowadays you don't even have to leave the house to get a support system. You can find people to connect with on social networking sites like Twitter and Facebook. There are online support groups for people who are miserable in their jobs or can't find a job, for people who suffer from an illness or are having trouble conceiving, for those who want to date, don't want to date, love their classic sports car . . . you name it, it's out there. Online support systems are easily accessible, so if you don't have a virtual one, it's likely because you haven't even looked or tried.

While encouraging you to seek connections online, I must also warn you that there is danger here, in the illusion of intimacy and the possibility of being deceived. When interfacing with someone online, the relationship may or may not be "real," and the other person may or may not be who he or she claims to be. Please be cautious in opening your heart, your home, or your pocketbook when it comes to anyone you have never met in person. Additionally, solid and real friendships and connections are built in real time—investing face time and energy getting to know who a person really is, how he lives his life and what he's all about. Obviously, there are inherent dangers in meeting people from online in real life—common sense applies! Don't go meet someone for the first time at his house or give your real address, and so on.

Another caveat to bear in mind as you find new people: water seeks its own level. A real grown up has a good idea of the kind of person she'd like to be and is constantly striving to become her best self. This journey is made much easier when your support system includes people who have achieved the kind of success you are wishing for—whether that's a happy marriage, a certain job title, or the level of financial success you want for yourself. Much like you see in sports teams and management teams, it is always better to measure yourself against a stronger person who forces you to up your game. You should spend as much time as possible investing in relationships with people you look up to and aspire to be like. That's the only way to raise your game. Your support network should contain people who are not only like you, but also outshine you.

If you are spending most of your time with people who are beneath you in social skills and motivation and who may not be as smart as you, you might feel good in the moment, but you are lacking the challenge to elevate to a higher level of social success. It's easy and comforting to spend time with people who have few expectations of you, and there's nothing wrong with doing so occasionally. It's a relaxing break. But when you spend the majority of time with people you consider successful and inspirational, you will aspire to be just like them!

CULTIVATE—Remember the saying "There's no free lunch"? It's true with people as well. You can't just ask people for things and favors all the time—you have to build a relationship, engage, connect, and bond. Use dynamic interaction! Relationships, like a garden, need to be cultivated to grow!

No one has time to cultivate everyone they meet. As you begin to become more conscious of all the people you meet and consider getting to know them better, you will realize fairly early on that they either have the potential to add to your life, neither add nor take away, or simply take away. When it comes to those who add to your life, you should be grateful for all they do, spend the most time with them, and value and appreciate their help most. You know you're going to get back as much as you give. The people who neither add nor take away are vanilla—they are pleasant to be around, they're fun to see, but your expectations should be kept to a minimum. Take-away people cost you time and energy and possibly even other friendships—at some point those people need to go. I would encourage you to focus your cultivation efforts toward those individuals and organizations that *add* to your life. After all, if you're going to be spending time and attention on something, shouldn't you be getting something back?

As you evolve and grow, you should nourish your friendships by taking your friends with you on your journey. For example, if you've lost a lot of weight and have begun living a healthy lifestyle, encourage them to join you. Or if you've gotten a great new job that has incredible perks, suggest they consider working in your industry. Or if you've discovered a new parenting program that's been successful for you, suggest they try it. Hopefully, they will come along and join you, and your bond and shared interests will become even stronger.

MAINTAIN—To become a high-functioning person who is maximizing your support network, you should realize that in order to maintain a quality relationship, you must commit to a steady flow of time and effort. Depending on that individual person or group, your output toward maintaining that connection may vary. Awareness of what the other person or group needs is a critical element in assessing what is needed to make that relationship long-lasting. Ask yourself: what do I need to do in order to leave the other person or persons fulfilled in this relationship? If I know what they desire, am I meeting their needs? What more can I do to ensure that we have a mutually beneficial relationship? Be aware that as time passes, not only do your needs change, but their needs change as well. Keep in close communication with them to make sure you are on top of their latest wants and needs and that you are fulfilling your role in their lives.

EVALUATE—Evaluating your support system is what I call "cleaning house." A grown up knows that in order to function well and be successful, there are times when you need to "clean house" when it comes to your support system. Instead of going through your things to see what you need and what you don't, you go through your people! Who's cluttering up your life and taking up too much space? Who has long been worn out—or has worn you out? Who's still useful and helpful? Who have you buried way back in a closet that you still like or need but haven't spent any time with in ages? And who do you wish you could stuff into a closet and not see ever again? It's important to look at who's still around and evaluate their needs and their usefulness in your life—the costs and the benefits—to see which outweighs which. The kinds of friends you happily spent all your time with in high school are not necessarily the people you want to spend time with as an adult. The coworkers you are more or less stuck interacting with at your job may not be at all the kinds of people you are drawn to spend time with in your free time.

As you evaluate, here's a rule you should live by: *no more fixer-uppers!* This is a common syndrome I see frequently enough to call "relationship potential glorification." This syndrome involves overlooking the reality of the person because you see past his or her bad behavior and hope to break through to that hidden diamond in the rough. Remember, this is your *support* system. You may have a very close relationship with somebody who actually is the complete opposite of supportive. The person may be critical, overbearing, tell you how to run your life, judge your choices, or be in constant crisis and demand far too much of your time and money; she doesn't destroy your life, but she doesn't add to it in any constructive manner. Maybe you've just gotten used to her personality or don't even realize how damaging this behavior is, but support, remember, means a soft place to land. Your circle needs to think you're great and continue to cheer you along a new and better path, not keep you stuck because of their own insecurities, not judge you and tell you that you can't.

There are plenty of people with good hearts and good intentions who will act badly and continually let you down. And I'm here to tell you that these good hearts and intentions are *not enough*. A real grown up judges her support system by their actions alone. Friends should be in your circle based on their behavior. You may be wasting time and energy on people who aren't maximizing your fulfillment and happiness, when you could be putting that time into new people who can add fuel to your desire to live a fully loaded life!

# Defining Your Friendship Categories

As you make new friends and reconsider your current circle, I believe you should recognize that there are different levels of relationships that can provide differing levels of support. It is important to know where people fall so you can adjust your expectations accordingly. As you read through each of the categories below, think about who in your life fits into which category so you know where your support system is strong and where it is lacking. This will help you figure out where work needs to be done.

## Two Degrees of Separation

People in this category are those you met through friends or work acquaintances. They're people you see at the same parties twice a year, or at the same business gatherings. Such a person might be your close friend's close friend or someone who works in the department adjacent to yours. It might be someone whom, if you saw him in a coffee shop, for example, you would stop to speak to or go over to say hello to. But that's as far as it has gone; no real relationship has been cultivated. These are people you could choose to reach out to, and they would likely respond to help you with your needs. Keep these people on your radar, because they might have the tools, resources, or connections you might need one day, and they could even become closer connections over time.

The perfect example of the benefits of the two-degrees-of-separation friendship is when you need a job, a nanny or babysitter, a good plumber, doctor, mechanic, and so on. I can't tell you how many times I have gotten an e-mail or phone call from a friend asking me if I have any suggestions or referrals for another friend of hers. As a matter of fact, the woman who babysat my children needed some extra work, and my friend Kathy called her friend Rikki and got the woman a job. Roll ahead eleven years later to to-day—Rikki is now *my* close friend, and our children are close too! As a matter of fact, that little two-degrees-of-separation friendship with Rikki led to my introduction to working in television! She shot and edited my first video, and her husband, Kevin, submitted it to get me my first television job! Oh . . . and it was Kevin who told me I should be writing this book. So in a sense, even you are being impacted by my relationship with them, and now, you are two-degrees-of-separation friends with them too!

## Legacy Relationships

This category may include a friend you've had since first grade or middle school. Maybe you've just reconnected with her online or at a reunion, or maybe you've stayed in touch through the years. This is the person who knew you when—and knows many of the historical details of your past. This is the person you call about high-school memories or when you're trying to get your college friends together. The great thing about legacy relationships is their foundation in your personal history; you have a lifelong connection with this person even if you no longer have anything in common. In all likelihood, this relationship is much more distant than it once was, and you have had less in common or more in common at different points through the years as life circumstances—moving, raising children—change.

Not everyone is fortunate enough to have been able to maintain a legacy relationship. Maybe you moved around too much, have changed so much that you no longer relate to anyone from your past, or have simply lost touch over time. I am blessed to still know my friend Leda from first grade. We met in the school orchestra in the percussion section. We bonded over the years talking about everything from how to play the finger symbols to which boys we wanted to date to how to raise our children. She is the one person in my life who knows a little something about everything from how badly I wanted a pair of designer jeans in middle school to my daily battle to avoid eating my favorite fattening food, French fries (her favorite food too!). The best part of legacy friends is that you never need to give them any backstory when something happens, because they were there all along.

## The New Relationship

This category means a possible friendship where you are just trying to lay the groundwork; you are still putting your best foot forward—and hopefully the other person is too! You're a bit nervous and edgy around this person, hoping to make the best possible impression because you admire him, believe spending time with him will help you develop personally and/or professionally. You are not sure what this relationship will develop into. This might be someone you met at work or in a class or through a friend. You want to be his friend, and you think he wants to be your friend too, but you're not sure where things are headed or how connected you two will become. This is the early groundwork of finding common interests and goals, exploring the connection, and getting to know that person better. These new relationships are exciting, because since the persons do not know you from your past, they will get to know the most recent you.

I've experienced this kind of relationship more than any other. Every new job, class, activity, or social situation presents this great opportunity to meet someone new. Perhaps it's because I am fascinated by other people and their stories, but I love the prospect of making new friends. That said, the development of a new relationship is always a challenge for me because I am so busy and want to make time for the friends I am already close with. I knew a friend who regularly had "bring a friend" potluck dinners at her house. Each guest she invited was charged with bringing a dish and a person whom the hostess didn't know to the evening. I thought this was a great way for her to expand her network and make new friends in a comfortable environment (her own home).

## Proximity Support Group

These are the people in your life who have become your friends because they are nearby. You have developed a relationship simply because you are thrown into contact with them—a next-door neighbor, a coworker, the person in your gym class. Because of frequency of contact, you have started to develop a relationship. This is the kind of person with whom you may have absolutely nothing in common and would never have sought out as a friend besides your shared activity, but she can actually turn into an enduring friend and support-system member. Because you share a similar space—gym, job, or neighborhood—her ability to support you might be customized to that particular area. She may know the ins and outs of your workout facility or the best dry cleaner in the area or who at the office could be a good resource for you. She may never see your house or meet any of your other friends, but you bond because you share a similar circumstance.

This is the group that you might pull together to do a weight-loss program, carpool, or neighborhood watch. You might ask one of them to watch your pet or child or take in your mail and newspaper while you're on vacation. In my case, this was the group I utilized as a child to make money. Around age seven, I sold my neighbors and people from my school tickets to my so-called performances where for fifty cents they could watch me jump on a trampoline while playing dance music. I also offered my hand-painted rocks as performance souvenirs for twenty-five cents. I had found a niche in the neighborhood, as I was the only kid offering this unique experience.

## Social Circle

These are the people you consider your day-to-day, week-to-week friends. You communicate with them on a regular basis and make time to see them face-to-face regularly. They know what's going on in your life, and you keep up with what's going on in theirs. The relationships are a constant give-and-take. These are the people with whom you likely have a great deal in common, have developed a history, and appear likely to have a future with as well. By the way, this is the category of friendship where the most gossip tends to take place. Since you are all such good friends, everyone in the group is inclined to discuss everyone else—in part to connect with one another and to keep up to speed on one another's lives.

In my neighborhood a group of us moms help one another out on a regular basis. To get out once in a while, we started a tradition of going together to breakfast or lunch to celebrate our birthdays. With life being so busy, this has been a great way to stay connected a few times a year. Similarly, another group of friends and I do a monthly Mexican dinner where we catch up on one another's lives. I've become so habituated to going to meet them that when we can't get together, I miss it!

## Your Person

I like to think that everyone has that one special person—though some have more than one "best friend." This is your most intimate friend—the one whom you trust with every secret, who knows every detail of your problems and who always seems to know just what to say. This is often a spouse or mate, a relative, or an official best friend. This is the one to whom you immediately want to tell any good or bad news—and when you can't reach this person, you feel like you're going to explode. Losing this person would be a devastating loss; this is your most trusted confidante. If you are fortunate enough to have such a person in your life, you enjoy the comfort of knowing that there is always someone in your corner.

If you have any question about who this person might be in your life, the story goes like this: she loves you and accepts you no matter how you look or what you've said or done day after day, week after week, month after month. When you call her in need, she makes time no matter how busy she is, and you do the same in return.

Earlier we discussed the importance of having a reliable mirror—one who usually falls into the "your person" category. As a reminder, that mirror is the person who serves the function of reassuring you that you are behaving appropriately or, if you are out of line, will throw a bucket of cold water in your face if need be to make sure she gets through. She can read over your presentations, help you clean up at your party, give you trusted advice about a mutual friend, and will gently tell you when what you are wearing makes you look fat. She will give you a ride, float you a loan, insist on taking you out on your birthday, and listen to you complain and complain about the same things over and over and over. Even when it comes to assessing your support system, you need that critical one person to tell you whether or not you're on track!

If you are reading and wishing that you had one of these friends who does all of these things for you, I would encourage you to put the most effort into this category to find or upgrade at least one person who will fit the bill. If you have your one trusted person to share all of the best and the worst with, then oftentimes, when it comes to support, that may be all you need.

**People will shift in and out of these various categories as time** passes and friendships evolve. The woman you meet at the gym each day could become your best friend. A coworker from an earlier job might become your dearest friend. Somebody with whom you have a casual relationship might steer you into a job where you become close colleagues for years. It's possible to develop a great independent friendship with someone who started as a two-degrees-of-separation person.

You can certainly downgrade friendships as well—whether because the proximity is lost, interests change, they just don't suit your needs, or a falling out was too great to repair. Your best friend at one point might become someone just in your regular circle or, even worse, your archenemy. Easily, the most painful breakup is when you lose "your person" against your will for whatever reason—it's a support-system divorce, with all the agony that accompanies that. When you lose all the things she brought to the table, it's just as bad as a romantic breakup or even worse. You have hopefully developed at least a couple of other people in other categories to fall back on in this case.

## It's Still About *You* First

The most important thing to keep in mind about your support system is that fully loaded grown ups don't *need* their support systems to run their lives. They are capable of functioning on their own and managing their own affairs most of the time. Your support system

| UPGRADE a Friend | DOWNGRADE a Friend |
| --- | --- |
| Offer to help her with something important to her. | Get married or involved in a relationship and ignore your friends. |
| Invite her to your home. | Move. |
| Get two friends who don't know each other together for lunch. | Talk behind your friend's back to a gossipy mutual friend. |
| Introduce your spouse/partner/kids to the new friend. | Work through lunch hour instead of eating with office friends. |
| Offer resources: money, time. | Block e-mails; ignore calls. |

steps in when you need a place to lean, some help, encouragement, or support. A real grown up's support system is not there to do it all for you, because it's better for you if it doesn't. Your greatest power and strength come from victories you achieve on your own, with your support system standing by to lift you as you fall and cheer while you rise up. Your support system enhances your life, gives you people to have fun with, play with, talk with, exchange confidences with, bounce ideas off.

If you are someone who excels in this area and are considered the ultimate support for people in your life, you may find that needy people and those who feel incapable or powerless are drawn to you. Why? Because you've got your life reasonably together and are healthy and high-functioning, so they think you can make their lives that way too! They may see you as a savior, a rescuer, someone who will do it all for them. This is the neighbor who sees that you seem to be doing a great job with your family life, so she assumes you'll raise her kids too; or the coworker who assumes you'll complete most of her tough assignments, because you're so smart and on the ball at the office. These people have the expectation that you'll handle their stuff for them, because you're clearly so much more capable.

Take care that you do not become a doormat of sorts for these weaker people because it's something that comes easily to you. No quality relationship lasts when the support is one-sided. Whatever category any of the members of your system falls into, it must be a give-and-take where both sides are reasonably happy; otherwise, one or the other will eventually burn out.

Most people have different friends they turn to for their various activities, troubles, and issues. You might have a person you turn to for advice about a problem at work. You confide in your oldest friend about your dating life. You turn to your mate to discuss family problems. If you're lucky, you will have one or two people in your life who fill many of these roles—"your person"—and you turn to him or her for everything. Oftentimes there's a customization when it comes to friends; each serves a role. The athletic friend you work out with, the party friends you see for drinks, your work friends who help you with projects. It's important to have a variety for all the different facets of your life so no one gets too bogged down dealing with everything about you.

A fully loaded grown up ideally has people in all these categories. They cultivate their support system constantly while maintaining valuable relationships and discarding destructive ones. They give back to their friends and know that what is given out will eventually be returned. A real grown up knows when it's time to lean on her network and when it's time to express gratitude to them for being there. There may come a time when you are unable to drag yourself out of bed or get that paper done or decide where to move or are having serious marriage troubles. A real grown up knows when its time to call in the troops. It's finding that balance between handling your own problems and reaching out for help that demonstrates your grown-up status.

## When Disaster Strikes

Research everywhere shows that when people have undergone a crisis, whether it's addiction, a messy divorce, trouble with a kid, a natural disaster like a hurricane or earthquake, or the serious illness of a child—they heal faster and move forward more easily if they rally a support system together and lean on it. That might mean a support group such as AA or Toughlove parenting program or a weight-loss group. It could be a neighbor, coworker, or friend; it might be a stranger you meet sitting in a meeting, or your longtime best friend. You will have to reach out and ask for help, which is something many "grown ups" find hard to do. See, the irony about all of this is that many of us have a great support system in place, but we just don't tend to make use of it. Do you utilize the resources and people around you? Or are you someone who says, "I don't want to put anyone out," "I hate to ask," "They're so busy with their own problems, they don't have time for mine," or, "I'm not worthy of getting help; I don't have enough to offer in return."

Real grown ups have a plan in place and secure help from their networks ahead of time. They know if they're planning a huge party in July, they need to book their friends in advance. They know if they have a tough work deadline next month, they call their work-adviser friends and schedule time with them to get help. They enable their friends to be acceptable and available to them, without constant crises and last-minute unreasonable requests.

In the coping chapter we talked about how it's important to tell as many people as possible your story when something traumatic happens to you. This is also applicable to support systems, because if you don't have people to tell when you have a crisis, you're going to have fewer people to help you and fewer shoulders to cry on. Building a strong support system helps every other category— coping (people to listen to your story and help you out), money (they could help you find a new job, improve your skills, teach you to balance a checkbook), and intimate relationships (it can take the pressure off of your romantic partner as you have other important people to lean on when times get tough.)

## Are All Your Eggs in One Basket?

Certainly one of the main reasons most of us want to get married or enjoy a committed relationship is that we are seeking the person who not only loves, accepts, and supports us, but can serve all of these support functions in one package. One of the traps people fall into is that they believe their spouses or romantic partners should not only meet all their sexual and intimacy needs, but also be their entire support system in every single area. Although that is a perfect ideal, in real life that is usually just not possible. Perhaps the person you've fallen in love with is in a completely different field and cannot help or advise you in your work or feels competitive if you work in the same field. That person cannot relate to your pile of paperwork or your kind of boss or the unique stresses of your

88

profession or project. Your spouse or partner may have absolutely no interest in your main passion in life—whether that's reading books, shopping, cooking, or camping and fishing and spending a lot of time outdoors. Sometimes a partner can be overwhelmed by his or her own responsibilities and interests and simply does not have the time to be there for you as often as you'd like. Maybe he or she has little tolerance for listening to you rattle off all of the details of a story or is tired of your staying friends with someone you constantly complain about.

Not only should you not expect your partner to become the be-all and end-all when it comes to support, he simply may not have it in him to give. You need to be able to fill these needs elsewhere instead of getting hung up and disappointed that your spouse or boyfriend doesn't give you "enough." We've all heard the saying, "Don't put all your eggs into one basket." The other problem with doing so, of course, is the potential loss of a spouse who is your be-all and end-all and complete and total support system; such a loss will be absolutely devastating, whether the relationship ends in divorce or death. If and when a mate who has been your one and only person for everything leaves, what, exactly, are you left with?

Everyone is familiar with a common phenomenon: when people enter into an intimate relationship, they push everyone else in their support group away. They no longer have the time and energy to devote to others; they become completely wrapped up in their romantic relationship. Real grown ups maintain a sense of balance—they cultivate their romantic relationship but continue to maintain their friendships. Of course, especially at the beginning of a new romance, you may not spend as much time with your friends. That's understandable when love is overwhelming and all-consuming. But a fully loaded grown up keeps in mind all the people who were there for her when she didn't have somebody. She includes them in her new life and doesn't drop them the minute a potential partner comes along.

**So many people who don't have a good support system appear** to be puzzled as to why, or they put up with a support system that, quite frankly, stinks. It's because they haven't worked hard enough on one or all of these areas: FIND, CULTIVATE, MAINTAIN, and EVALUATE. Part of being a real grown up is having some sense of awareness. Learn to build, maintain, and grow nourishing relationships. The minute you walk into a new environment, start thinking about what you want and need in your life, and start finding/cultivating the people who embody those things!

The great benefit of being an adult is that, unlike during your childhood, your friendships can be on your terms. As a grown up, you get to make the rules. You are free to spend as much or as little time as you please with whomever you choose, doing whatever activities you desire.

You will read many times in this book about the importance of having a great support system. This group of people is critical for leaning on in bad times and uplifting in good times. When you are in need or facing problems, these people can offer resources and pick you up when you're down. When you have a great victory, half the joy is telling people who will celebrate your success. Now that you know the types of supportive relationships there are, think about the ones you are in need of most, and then go connect with someone as fabulous as you are!

# I Don't Care If You Have Bad Breath ... Kiss Me Anyway!

**A**fter spending nearly twenty years as a therapist, if I broke out the various issues that my clients have come to see me about or I get asked about on television, their root is almost always their relationships with other people. Some want to address long-standing issues with parents or siblings that continue to affect their adult lives, others want to learn how to parent more effectively. Some come to explore an addictive or destructive behavior that is adversely affecting their lives and relationships or to learn some tools to better handle an impossible boss or work situation. But most often what drives people to actually seek out my guidance is their concern about intimate relationships and the issues in and around finding and maintaining one. When we're talking about how to have a happy, fulfilling lifestyle, this category seems to be near the top of the list.

It is still startling to me, even though I have experienced it myself, that a satisfying love relationship has the power to make you the happiest and most productive you've ever been or so miserable and unproductive that you want to bury yourself under the covers and never come out! If the person you spend the most time with, invest the bulk of your efforts and energy toward, and hold to the highest standards is continually disappointing you or failing to meet your needs, this dissatisfaction can trickle into every other area of your life. Or if you long for an intimate relationship and launch a full-force effort into finding one—whether that involves going to bars, joining online dating sites, finding that perfect outfit, reading relationship books, or taking classes in hopes of finding "*the one*," and none of these strategies succeed—it can be at minimum distracting to your life and at maximum throw you into a full-blown state of depression or anxiety, leaving you with a domino effect of troubles!

On top of what I have encountered in my day-to-day life as a therapist about everyone's desire to find quality relationships, I read an amazing statistic in the *Wall Street Journal*, August 19, 2005: the single largest chunk of American households now consists of people who live alone. No spouse, no partner, no kids or other relatives, no roommate or boarder. Alone. Specifically, more than 27 million adults live all by themselves—a fairly recent and surprising demographic trend. The great irony, of course, is that nearly every one of us seems to long to enjoy a loving, caring partnership, but these days it has become more and more challenging to have one. The divorce rate is up, men and women are trying to juggle job pressures and relationships, most couples have two careers they are coordinating around, children put tremendous stress on the strongest relationships, tough economic times leave people feeling stressed and agitated, and now more than ever we have all become pickier and pickier about who we want to spend our time with. So, many of us are left alone, without a partner to share our home, our time, our joys, and our sorrows.

Falling in love is easy, but grown-up relationships are hard work, and it's tough to find somebody in the first place, let alone remain happily partnered over the long term. Here's my take: We all want a love relationship, but we hope and secretly expect that it will be easy. I mean, come on, wouldn't it be great to just love someone and have them love you back without any conflict, tension or drama? Even as grown ups we all share the fantasy that true love is enough; because we love each other so much everything else will fall into place. Love is all that should matter. The unfortunate truth is that love as we define it—that explosive feeling that gushes out of your heart or that quiet peaceful adoration of another—is never enough. The current divorce rate is close to 60%, and there's a good reason for that. It's because these intimate relationships are by far the toughest relationships to maintain!

The love that IS enough is what I want you to experience in your life. I call it "lasting love." But before I tell you what is needed to find and keep lasting love, let me first point out what it is not. Lasting love is not what we feel when we've just met someone or are in a new relationship and experience the constant, intense desire to be close to them and to rip their clothes off. That feeling is lust and comes out of passion and chemistry—which, by the way, feels fantastic and is ideal in lasting love too, but I'll explain more about that in a bit. Nor is lasting love that worshipful indebted feeling you get when someone has helped you out of a painful or traumatic situation, and you suddenly look at them with such admiration that you feel like you might be falling in love. That feeling comes out of gratitude and appreciation, also important factors in lasting love, but not enough to stand the test of time. It is also not that excitement you feel when you discover that this person drives your favorite car, has an amazing house in a neighborhood that you have always wanted to live in, or has a ton of money and buys you everything you ask for. All of these are great perks, of course, but that is called infatuation and is based on what the person has and gives you and not who they are.

Lasting love unites the passion from chemistry, the adoration from your heart, and the sensibility of your mind. It requires respect, dedication, trust, hard work, and dynamic communication. Ironically, most of the couples who approach me for help with their relationship both want exactly the same things at their core. They want to be close, they want to have a harmonious drama-free partnership, they each want the other person to treat them with kindness and respect, and they want to enjoy some passion. Somehow, despite their shared desire to be happy together, they may not be getting any of those things, or may intensely feel like the one thing they aren't getting is tearing them apart. When it comes to finding or creating a long-lasting romantic relationship, even the smartest and most together (in every other area of their lives) men and women often cannot seem to figure out how to make it work. They're just stumped: puzzled about how they can be so strong in some areas and so challenged in this key area. The purpose of this chapter is to help you solve the puzzle, to give you an understanding of what a lasting love relationship is, what it takes to find and maintain it, and to help you see some of the obstacles that might be in your way.

As a grown up, it is your job to take responsibility for your own heart and your own happiness. I have often heard people say that "the heart wants what the heart wants," as if they have no choice in the matter and no ownership over their feelings and desires. It is absolutely up to you to protect your own heart, because the heart doesn't have a brain of its own—it can't think, weigh out pros and cons, or reason with itself. The heart feels and longs and desires and can be badly broken when you don't take on the responsibility to look out for it. That said, hearts still get broken even when we do our best to manage and protect ourselves, but it is our job to do all we can to take care of what is ours.

\* \* \*

**At the beginning of this book, in the dynamic communication** chapter, we talked about the most important relationship there is— the one with yourself. This is the one area in your life where you have complete and total control and power. Every other kind of interaction involves other people and your relationships with them— friends, coworkers, neighbors, etc. You can't control these other people. You can influence them, if you're lucky, but ultimately, you can discard or distance yourself quite easily from many of the people in your life. You can find a new job or keep so occupied at work that you avoid and distance yourself from irritating coworkers. You can connect with a different person to have lunch with or find replacement friends for shopping trips.

Things aren't so easy with an intimate relationship, because typically it is here you have likely become the most attached, invested the most, and will find it to be the most difficult relationship to replace. On top of that, you have to struggle balancing the very human desire for power and control against what's best for you, what your partner wants, and what ultimately benefits your relationship. Most of us struggle to find that balance. We tend to either focus too much on demanding what *we* want, or we bend over backward trying to accommodate what our partner wants. Either of those could leave you in a position where you are not only *not* doing what's best for *you*, but you may also be damaging what is best for the relationship as a whole. So let's begin where I always say that we should, the place where you hold the ultimate power and control—with you.

First, let's take an honest look at a feeling that greatly impacts the search and maintenance of most intimate relationships and prevents you from finding lasting love. That feeling is *fear*. Fear of being alone, fear of intimacy, fear of rejection, fear of picking wrong, fear of being judged, fear of conflict, fear of asking for and not getting what you want, fear of leaving, fear of the unknown, fear of being dumped, fear of not being enough, fear of what your family or friends will say, fear of settling . . . the list of potentially scary things is long enough to fill an entire book! What are your particular fears? What has gotten in your way? Fear is an unpleasant feeling, which most of us do our best to bury or minimize so we don't have to face it. But grown ups take a moment to look at what's in their way so they can analyze the issues, learn from their pasts, and avoid future mistakes. So that's why I'm asking you to take a moment to consider what fears you have. Note: many of us at this point might immediately begin to think about the fears of our partner or past partners so that we can better understand them. That is fine, but only after you have first examined yourself. Remember, this book is about *you* and what *you* can change to better impact your life. Other people come second.

Ask yourself the following questions about what scares you most now or has in the past: Do you make every decision in relationships because you are afraid to give up control? Does fear cause you to have unrealistic expectations of or make unreasonable demands on a partner? Are you the type who fears conflict to the point that you bend over backward so that your partner will like you better? Does fear prevent you from asking for what you want? If you do ask and don't receive, do you give up? start a fight? retreat? walk away? Any and all of these reactions come out of fear—that fight or flight response that keeps us from thinking things through and causes us to react immediately instead.

Fear is a scary feeling that many of us don't understand how to manage. What should you do when fear is immobilizing you, leaving you wanting to retreat, or making your head spin? The answer comes best in the story about you and a fire. If you were in a burning house with flames around you and someone you love and care for was outside waiting for you, what would you do? Would you grab a magazine and sit down and read? No. Would you spend the next twenty minutes debating whether or not to escape? I hope not. Would you jump up and down having a temper tantrum about the fact that your loved one is outside of the building and you are not? I doubt it. You would move. You would do what you could to get out. Not only to be reunited with your loved one, but to benefit your own well-being. Fear in a relationship is very much the same. You need to face your fear and do what is best despite the fear. You can take baby steps, you can run as fast as you can, but you must act.

Now that we have briefly examined fear, we need to talk about a second barrier to finding lasting love: relationship baggage. As an adult, you have more than likely been involved in a serious relationship or even marriage. Hopefully you have learned a bit about yourself and your weak spots. Whether you have or haven't learned some lessons, if you've had a relationship fail in the past, you will have relationship baggage. Relationship baggage comes from experiences and challenges in your past that impact your current relationships. It's as if your current situation or relationship is magnified so that you react more emotionally or dramatically because of what you've been through before. If you have been cheated on or cheated, you might have baggage related to trust. If you have been abandoned, you might have baggage that leaves you fearing that your new mate will pull the trigger and break your heart like the last one. If you have dated someone who put you low on the priority list of his life, you might have heightened sensitivity if your current partner ever engages in *any* activity that doesn't include you.

As if having this baggage isn't challenging enough, add to it the fact that baggage can cause what I call "recycled feelings." Recycled feelings are generated by our baggage and cause us to bring old emotions into the new union. We play those old feelings over and over like luggage rotating on a carousel. These old feelings can cause us to sabotage our current relationship for no legitimate reason. For example if you have been cheated on, taken advantage of, smothered, ignored, or even simply dumped unexpectedly when you thought everything was fine, you might take those feelings from your past and re-create them in a new relationship. You begin to overthink the current situation over and over and over again recycling the feelings and can become hypervigilant, anxious, worried, dramatic, depressed, or edgy—these feelings are the recycled ones. Think hamster on a wheel, round and round your emotions go, and when they will stop, no one knows. These repetitive thoughts and feelings from your old relationships may cause you to run scared—and may even lead you to break up with your new love too soon.

We've talked in past chapters about the voices in your head, and never are they louder than when it comes to romantic relationships. I've noticed that some well-adjusted people can actually control these voices that warn: *He's way too good-looking, he's going to leave me*; *My last girlfriend cheated, so this one will too*; *The last time I dated an Italian, or a tall guy, or someone from work* . . . and refuse to allow their minds to go into overdrive. For most of the rest of us, however, it's a struggle to turn these voices off and deal with the actual person who is right in front of us and his real-life current behavior. I would encourage you to spend some time thinking about what baggage you carry from your past, what recycled feelings still impact your emotions, and remain conscious of them so you can do your best to keep *both* of those out of your current and future relationships as much as possible.

## Want Versus Need

Now it's time to look at what you need and want from your partner. If you don't know in clear detail what you desire, how on earth can you expect anyone else to know? There is a difference between what you need and what you want. Needs are the must have, necessary, can't-live-without qualities and traits, while wants are the desired but could-manage-without things. Needs and wants change with time, age, and circumstance and need to be reevaluated throughout your life. I find that people don't give enough consideration to what they *need*, but instead frequently settle for what they want. Let's say you need somebody who is attentive and communicative, but what you have is somebody who has an interest in hiking, swimming, and outdoor activities—just like you. You two can get by for a good amount of time because you have common interests and have fun together and busy yourselves with all kinds of activities. But at the end of the day, when you're having a rough time, this person may not be there in the way that you *need*—when you're not swimming or hiking or camping but dealing with day-to-day irritations and major crises. It's crucial to get clear on what your *needs* are, because a real grown up knows the difference between wants and needs. Wants are negotiable; needs are not. Below I have an exercise to help you sort out your needs and wants at this moment in time. Plan to do this exercise again in the future as you get older or your life changes. You will see how much your priorities will change over time!

Make a list of what you *need* from your intimate relationship:

(Examples: I need someone with a job, someone who treats me with respect, is trustworthy, motivated, driven, kind, has similar interests; someone who wants/likes kids, someone whom my family and friends like, someone who adores me and treasures me and thinks I'm amazing and funny, who will like/spend time with my friends, who has the same interests as I have.)

Make a list of what you *want* from your intimate relationship:

(Examples: I want someone who likes to exercise, but I can do that with a friend—I don't *need* it. I want someone who is in a similar profession, but if he has a totally unrelated job, I can live with it. I want someone who is taller than I, but I'm willing to be open enough to date someone shorter. I want someone who shares my interest in cooking, playing tennis, reading, etc.)

**Paying close attention to the baggage from your past, knowing** that many of us tend to recycle feelings, making a concerted effort to separate out your old relationship baggage from the new relationship, and knowing the difference between "wants" and "needs" are surefire ways to increase the likelihood of your new relationship being a lasting love!

**Have you ever met someone who seems to have all of the luck in** love? Maybe you even happen to be that person! You know the one—like the person I'll write about in the chapter about jobs. He stumbles into some random job, it becomes his career and provides endless happiness and success. Well, those lucky ones exist in the relationship arena as well. Maybe he found his soul mate at a dinner party or coffee shop when he wasn't even looking. Or she woke up one day and realized her close friend of five years was someone special, got married right away, and went on to live happily ever after. Or he met his true love in junior high and never wanted or looked at another. Although those romantic happenings occur regularly in movies, fairytales, and television shows, and once in a while in real life, most of us just aren't that lucky. We need to spend the time and do the work to beat the odds. We less-lucky people need to develop a set of standards, expectations, desires, and limits, and then we need to get out there and actually *look!*

If you are currently unattached but actively seeking an intimate relationship—or claim that you are—are you spending enough time cultivating that desire? Many of us get more wrapped up in escaping into our televisions, talking to friends, or playing online than actually trying to *find* that special someone. Talking about your desire to have a relationship is one thing, but are you spending the necessary time and energy to get it? Or are you investing more time just talking and complaining about how you are relationship-less, your friends are behaving badly, how mean and unreasonable your boss is, how you never meet anyone, or that you're so busy at work that you only have ten minutes of free time a day?

Fully loaded grown ups don't just long for happiness or complain about not having it, grown ups take action toward getting what they want. They don't settle for being alone, they don't settle for the status quo, and they don't just take the first person who comes knocking at their doors. If both you and your current or potential partner are doing the same amount of work toward creating and maintaining a relationship, your chances of success are doubled!

**When it comes down to actually selecting that special someone,** people make choices from their hearts, their heads, or their hormones. When it comes to living a fully loaded life, grown ups know that ultimately they should be looking for a unity of all three. The ideal relationship has all of those elements: you are physically, emotionally, and intellectually fulfilled. If you settle for less—say, you choose someone who's perfect on paper because your mind alone is dictating, *I want somebody who is this religion, has this job, and wants kids*—it's great in theory, but lack of attraction and emotion will eventually take their toll. These holes will eventually impact your relationship because in the end there has to be passion, excitement, and chemistry, and there also has to be a rich emotional connection.

Earlier in this chapter, I asked you to list the qualities that you need in a relationship. I now challenge you to take that a step further and list what your head, your heart, and your body need individually, as if they were three separate entities—after all, when it comes to being happy, the more you know about yourself, the better!

**HEAD**

**HEART**

**BODY**

Once you have made the three lists, ask yourself the following questions: Am I getting (or did I get) what I need or most of what I need in all three areas from my current or past relationships? Do I tend to meet and date people who fulfill all three elements, or have I been investing time with those who are below the bar?

The biggest, most common failure I see in choosing a mate is not having a solid combination of all three of these elements. If you have all three, and one area is failing for the moment—such as your mate got busy, or physically ill, or overly emotional, or distant—you can fall back on the fact that the person is still meeting your needs in other areas, at least for a while. For example: if your mate does something to hurt you emotionally, but you have amazing chemistry with him and he satisfies your intellectual needs as well, you can talk yourself out of the hurt feelings and brush aside his forgetting your birthday or speaking rudely to you.

In any case, I'm sure that anyone you know who's found a successful intimate relationship will tell you that the greatest challenge comes after you've found that special someone and the two of you realize you need to work at sustaining the relationship in order for it to withstand the test of time. As a brilliant colleague once said to me, "For most of us, we get married and then we have to go to work." If you prioritize putting time and energy into your intimate relationship, there is no doubt in my mind that you'll reap the benefits of lasting love.

## It's All About Respect

When I ask people to talk about what they're looking for in an intimate relationship, they answer with things like: somebody I feel a connection with, a companion, great chemistry, funny, tall, employed . . . What I rarely hear people answer is, "Somebody who treats me with respect." To me, any successful intimate relationship is built on a foundation of respect. If you respect the person, you will always consider his feelings and needs, and you will know that he will do the same for you. A grown up is looking for someone who understands the value of respect and shows it to his or her family, coworkers, and romantic partner. When people are disrespectful to any of these others, there will come a day, no matter how fabulous they are to you now, when they will not respect you. If you are in a relationship now, or are seeking a relationship, the number one question to ask yourself is: *Do we have a strong foundation of respect?*

The way I describe respect came out of a definition I learned from my mentor Gloria Hirsch. My definition is as follows: respect means putting the comfort, well-being, and happiness of the person you're with equal to your own. If I am hungry and feel like having Italian food, but you want Chinese, I will consider both of our desires and work toward compromise. What to eat is a very superficial example, but the idea behind this choice extends out to even big decisions. If I want to live in the suburbs, and you want to live in the heart of the city, and I care about your comfort, feelings, and happiness, then we're going to do everything we can to make both of us happy. If I like sports and want to watch a game every night, but it makes my partner miserable, we're going to work out a way that we're both happy. Successful relationships have two partners who have built on a foundation of respect, where they put each other's needs equal to their own instead of above or below. I insist that if you have not listed respect in your list of needs in the earlier exercise, add it now. After all, I care about your finding a quality partnership, and I will guarantee that if you insist on receiving respect and give it in return you will increase your chance of success!

When I meet couples, whether it's in private practice or on television, seeing a lack of respect on either of their parts is the biggest red flag to me that they're on the path to a breakup. In my mind it is the biggest single indicator that things are not going well, and failure is in their future. Why is it that we treat the people we profess to love most the worst? A grown up shouldn't do that, and yet so many of us do. Sometimes we treat insignificant people—a clerk in a store that we'll never see again—with more respect and good manners than we do our own mates! We need to flip this tendency. If you can treat someone who hardly matters well, then you can treat somebody who really matters better.

We are told from a very young age that love is all about accepting you for who you are. That you are allowed to unload on your significant other, because he is "safe" and has to love you no matter what. How many times have you heard somebody say, "Everybody loves him; they think he's a great guy, but no one has any idea how horrible he is at home alone with me." We are tacitly told in a million ways that it's okay to treat the people we are closest to poorly, and we're all guilty of it. We don't elevate our partners to the proper level of their value in our lives, and I believe that's the first step everyone should take to improve an intimate relationship, and it's one of the most important items for you to insist on in your list of needs. If it isn't on your list—go add it now! By the way, this detail of being treated at a high level of consideration falls under the category of respect, which I had you add earlier. But I want it listed separately because I also consider it an indication of adoration, which I personally think is the second-most-important factor to have in an intimate relationship. Doesn't it sound wonderful to think of being respected and adored forever?

## The Cherry Pie Story

I once counseled a couple named Jill and John. They had only been dating for a short time, but they were very much enamored with each other. When Jill's birthday came up, John went to the store with the intention of surprising her with a fabulous dessert. As he stood in front of the bakery counter, he realized he had absolutely no idea what sweets Jill liked. It happened to be summertime, near the Fourth of July, so there was a huge display of cherry pies laid out. He thought, *I don't want to be predictable and be like everybody else. I'm not going to get her the standard birthday cake; I'm going to get her something special. I am going to buy her a cherry pie!*

Little did he know that not only did Jill not like pie, she hated cherries. John was so excited because he thought out of the box and did something creative and was already envisioning this as the start of a tradition. Every year, he thought, for her birthday he would buy her a cherry pie for them to share. He showed up at her house with a bunch of gifts and the pie hidden in a bag. She was delighted with the presents as each one was something she loved. Lastly, she opened up the bag with the pie, and her face fell. "What is *this?*" she asked.

"A cherry pie!" John said proudly.

"I *hate* cherries, and I hate pie! Who would ever choose a pie for a birthday dessert? You're crazy!" Without asking any questions or being open to his explanation, Jill told John to go home, and without hesitation he did.

Jill did not take the time to stop and listen to the rationale behind this gift. She reacted based on her (high) expectations and lashed out. If she had heard the story, she might have realized how sweet and well meaning John was. She only found that out two weeks later when they came to see me. They are married now. This incident with the cherry pie comes up every year. Even now, there's still clearly a lot of investment and emotion in it.

I share this story because although John is the only man I have ever met who has bought a cherry birthday pie, the underlying themes and issues are quite common in couples I meet. Many people in intimate relationships only consider their own interpretation of a partner's action, instead of trying to figure out what the other person is truly trying to say or do. They don't ask questions, they don't probe for details or an explanation, and often they spin their own tale as to why their mates did what they did or said what they said. It is important when your partner disappoints you or does something you don't like to do some investigation. You know, that legal presumption of "innocent until proven guilty" should also apply to your relationship!

An evolved dynamic communicator might say, "Gosh, a cherry pie. That's not my favorite, actually I don't really like them, and it's an unusual choice for a birthday . . . I'm wondering what you were thinking." Then she listens to the story before she reacts. Imagine what would have happened if Jill had asked John a question like that? I was the first person to ever ask him why the cherry pie, because I know that when somebody does something unusual or out of the ordinary, there's usually a reason.

**I've told you the two most important elements to have in a** relationship; now let me tell you some things that I see on a regular basis that can lead your relationship to a slow and sad end.

As we'll talk more about in the balance / time management chapter, we live in a society of instant gratification. These days relationships are very much about what I want here and now—today, right this minute—and that can be damaging to a partnership that you aspire to have last long term. Focusing on how you are not feeling happy right this minute takes the focus off of being happy in the end. If we want to walk together, holding hands into the sunset as a happy elderly pair, then we need to make the choices now in our relationship that lead in that direction.

I think you and I would agree that you desire more than just love, but lasting love. To attain that goal, stop the following behaviors immediately: give up the need to be right, the need to win, the finger-pointing, the name calling, the yelling, and the fights about the small stuff. Keep the end game firmly in mind: when we are old, I want us to still be together. People get too caught up in day-to-day demands and irritations and forget that there's a bigger goal of being together for a lifetime.

Plants need time and care, and yet the relationship that people give the least time and care to is the one they are closest to. If you are involved in an intimate relationship, do you spend time growing it, cultivating it, and maintaining it? Or are you too busy? That is where the idea of respect comes in. If everything you do is based on respect, wanting your partner to be happy while adoring him in the process, then you've done 60 percent of the work already. Naturally most people fall far short of even this. They stop trying. They put work first. Sports first. The kids' needs. They scream and yell. They snipe or give the silent treatment. They argue over little things, when most of these things could be worked out if they love each other and are committed to the relationship.

What else gets in the way of intimate relationships? The two deadly Ps: pride and power. Both are healthy, desirable qualities in ourselves and others—when properly demonstrated and not used to beat others over the head! People with pride generally care about their work, results, and reputation, and they tend to look and perform at their highest level. Pride also keeps them from being abused or taken advantage of. Power is a great thing to have—this whole book is about personal power!—as long as it is exercised benevolently and for the greater good—not to abuse and take advantage of another. The problems with the two deadly Ps come when they are used as weapons to alienate, get leverage, or push people away. The ultimate result: distance and conflict between you and the person on the receiving end of your prideful and overpowering ways.

Pride says, *I'm too good for this*. Pride says, *I'm not giving this to you, because you don't give it to me*. Pride says, *You did this, so I'm doing that*. Pride says, *I'd rather win than give in*. Its cousin, power, comes along hand-in-hand with pride. Power says, *Winning is more important than peace*. Power says, *I don't have to listen to you*. Power says, *What I say should go. Period*. Power says, *I don't care what you want as long as I get what I want*. Remember the whole idea to keep in mind of walking together as two elderly people holding hands into the sunset?

Fortunately, these battles for pride and power tend to wane with age. Many people, as they get older, tend to soften. They become more fragile and less invested in their egos. Their pride and the desire for power are no longer their primary driving forces. They're just as happy to hold hands and play shuffleboard. Remember this *now*!

## The Ultimate Prize

My whole point in writing this book is to encourage you. To make you want to behave in a grown-up way, because the rewards are so worth it, and to give you some tools to set you on the right path in every area! Like everything else we've discussed so far in this book, the skills to navigate intimate relationships can be learned, no matter how dismal your romantic history. It is not too late to change, grow, and learn.

Unfortunately, however, some change involves pain. Given the overwhelming tendency to head down the wrong path—meaning, fall in love with the "wrong" person—that we've all been guilty of at one time or another, what can we do about that *now*? This is where we have to walk the talk when it comes to being a fully loaded grown up. A grown up knows that *the right thing to do is often the hardest thing to do!* Whether this means walking away from a long marriage, giving up on an addicted boyfriend or girlfriend no matter how much the person loves you and begs you to stay, recognizing early on that your needs aren't being met while you're dating somebody and breaking up with them, and so forth. Yes, it's painful and difficult. Yes, making this kind of informed decision is the downside to being a grown up. But in some cases there is simply no chance for mutually fulfilling lasting love, and that's what this chapter is all about.

I've talked a great deal about laying the foundation to build and maintain a successful, lasting love relationship. I'd like to leave you with what I call the 4 Cs of quality relationship building that integrate the importance of respect, adoration, dynamic interaction, and conflict management: Consider, Compromise, Comfort, and Compliment.

> **CONSIDER** your partner's feelings, thoughts, and desires. Insist your partner consider yours as well.

> **COMPROMISE** as often as you can. If you are both happy/satisfied, you both win. Choose a partner who is interested in compromising as well.

> **COMFORT** your partner when he or she is in pain, even if it's because of something you did. Your partner deserves it, because we all deserve it, and deserves it even more because you love each other. Don't settle for a partner who can't comfort you in return.

> **COMPLIMENT** daily. It lifts people up, puts a smile on their faces, counteracts insecurities, makes up for the challenges they've had or mistakes they've made, and it simply feels good! Find someone who sees value in complimenting you back!

As children, our fairytales all ended the same way: "They got married and lived happily ever after." These childhood stories were written by other people. Now that you're a grown up and creating the story of your own life, you get to write your own happy ending!

# 6

# Does This Chapter Make Me Look Fat?

**W**hen my oldest daughter was three years old, she fell in love with a pair of sparkly ruby red "Dorothy" party shoes and insisted on wearing them everywhere with everything. This meant that on most days her shoes did not remotely match her outfit. She painted in them, ran races in them, wore them to parties with a fancy dress, to the pool and beach with her bathing suit, and to the playground with shorts and a T-shirt. If you asked her, she'd tell you enthusiastically that her sparkly red shoes were perfect with any outfit and that she looked great as long as she wore them—and she was right! The best thing about those shiny red shoes was that they made my daughter feel great. She walked taller. She sang louder. She ran faster (and occasionally slid from the lack of traction). But mostly those slippers impacted who she was and how she felt about herself in a very positive way, and that was all that mattered.

When she grew out of ruby slippers and started playing Little League, her younger sister used to come along to watch her games. Following in her big sister's footsteps, she developed a style all her own. Only this daughter of mine outfitted herself in a baseball jersey and baseball cap—accompanied by a pink tutu! Oh, and she often topped off the look fully loaded up with lip gloss! Sometimes

I suspected that everyone was looking at us because my daughter's getup was silly; she thought they were looking at her admiringly because she was high-fashion fabulous! Friends and strangers would giggle and smile and point, but since my daughter assumed that people were doing that as a compliment, she felt great!

Now, if any of you at this point are thinking about buying ruby red dress shoes or pairing some athletic wear with a tutu—feel free! But this chapter is not about offering you fashion tips; it's about showing you how your appearance—and, more important, how you feel about your appearance—is a barometer of how you feel you fit into the world. We all know someone who may not be the thinnest or the best-looking person, yet she puts herself together well, radiates confidence, and looks and seems to feel fabulous. It's not about how the person actually looks, but how she believes she looks, much like what was going on with my daughters. This chapter is about finding that feeling, as a grown up, that my daughter had as a child—in a socially and sartorially acceptable way! My mission is for you to radiate that same level of confidence, and you can do that no matter what you wear or how objectively attractive you might be.

**From the moment we are born, others judge and comment on** our appearance, because there's nothing else to remark upon—we haven't yet developed personalities. What a beautiful baby! She has eyes just like her mommy! Who does he look like, Mom or Dad? Oh, no, Grandma's ears! Our height and weight are even the very first official facts sent to our family and friends on our baby announcements. The comments about our appearance begin the second we make our entrance into the world and continue until the day we die.

It's impossible to talk about appearance without talking about mirrors. There are two kinds of mirrors we encounter in our lives: the actual mirrors we look into to see our reflection, and the mirrors that are the people who reflect back to us who we are and how we look. Family and friends are our first such reflecting mirrors; they are the people who first tell us, "Oh my gosh, you're so tall!" or "What a chubby belly!" The two types of mirrors are everywhere, whether it's a bathroom or compact mirror, or people telling you for as long as you can remember, "You're pretty," or, "You have great hair," or teasing you about your huge nose. All of this feedback sets a foundation for how you see yourself.

As we grow older, people continue to remark on family resemblances: you may strongly take after one parent or another—or neither, and everyone tries to figure out where that red hair and those freckles came from. These statements affect how we see ourselves fitting into our environment, but the greatest impression is left by the attitudes about looks that our parents or caregivers convey. Some parents put their own needs before their child's self-esteem— they care more about how they feel about a child's appearance and style than how he or she feels about it. They focus more on whether or not the child's clothes match than wanting her to feel good because she picked out green shoes to match her orange pants and pink shirt. To some degree all parents make statements through their children based on what they want people to see and what they themselves like, though some take it to extremes.

Some celebrities give their babies Mohawks or matching haircuts to look just like theirs, or dress them in the particular line of clothes they design. It is not likely that these kids are asking for this; yet the parents are imposing their sense of style or appearance on their children. A parent who is worried that no one will know that her adorable bald baby is a girl tapes a pink ribbon to her head.

Some parents think that they have to dress their kids in the most expensive, latest fashions, out of fear they won't look cute or fit in if they don't have the right bloomers or oxford shirt. This behavior reflects how much parents are invested in what the world is thinking about their child's appearance.

Around the age of two or three, children start to form definite opinions: "I don't want to brush my hair!" "I won't wear that shirt!" "I only wear blue!" As kids get older and start spending more time with their peers at school, they begin to want to develop their own styles based on what the latest trends are in their peer group. They start splitting off into certain cliques: preppy, grungy, or following the crowd and wanting to look like everybody else. This is a critical time where parents who are pushing their own agendas too hard can wind up with a child who rebels in terms of appearance—tattoos, piercings, extreme haircuts or dye jobs; any sort of look the parents hate—or doesn't have any real sense of who she is and how she wants to look and dress.

Up until the age of nine or ten, many kids don't really care too much how they look. Parents are begging them to wash up, take showers, comb their hair, and put on a clean shirt. Around the onset of puberty, all of a sudden they become very conscious of how they look to other people. Adolescence means paying way too much attention to how they look; this is when they start spending all their time in the bathroom, fixing their hair, going through their closets over and over and not finding anything decent to wear, and agonizing about how "ugly" or "fat" they are. It's not easy on anyone, but hopefully we, and they, survive adolescence and high school without any lasting damage or severe trauma to their self-esteem.

Added to what took place in our upbringing, society is hyperfocused on outward appearance and celebrity—that's just a fact of modern life. Entire magazines and television shows and newscasts are devoted to what designer clothes the stars are wearing, who lost her baby weight fastest, what's the coolest new accessory, how you can get the same beautiful hair or skin a star has. There are books, programs, television shows, blogs, newsletters, and breaking news stories on how to get thinner, have toned abs, and look younger. Ads for Botox, Restylane, implants, creams, potions, and tonics entice you to look fresher, firmer, less saggy, and wrinkle free. You could spend all of your free time engaging in some activity to improve your appearance in some cosmetic way. This intense focus on appearance and youth and the pressure to achieve physical perfection can lead even the most secure person to become caught up in such concerns as, what new outfits had I better buy this season? what's the latest, most politically correct car to drive? why doesn't my house look like the ones in the magazines? does my child have the right clothes to fit in at school? All of this can just be background noise to our daily lives—sometimes subtle but always insidious. Other times it sounds like a full-blown marching band playing "Are you too fat?" and "What on earth are you wearing?" loudly in our ears.

It doesn't matter where you live, how much income you have, whether you are a stay-at-home mom or a business executive—there are people looking, judging, and evaluating details of your appearance and what it announces to the world every day. The purpose of this chapter is to encourage you to become less affected by their judgment and more focused on your desired vision with regard to your appearance.

I walk into my children's school performance and hear the chatter of mommies saying things like, "You look so pretty" to the mom who typically roams around in sweats with her hair in a sloppy ponytail and no makeup, because she appears to have showered, her hair is combed, and she isn't wearing something with stains all over it. I walk into a business meeting to hear one woman say to another, "What a great pair of shoes; are they new?" before the topic of the business at hand is even discussed. These remarks are made as a way to connect, compliment, and build rapport, but they highlight the fact that everyone who can see, looks and judges. There's no escaping it: how we appear to the outside world is noticed and often remarked on.

I moved into a neighborhood that is known for having great schools and being family and community oriented. After my daughter's first day of kindergarten, I called her new friend's mommy to arrange a playdate. After introducing myself and letting her know what I was calling about, she said, "You seem nice. You should know that there are three types of moms in this neighborhood: the 'beautiful people'—the moms who get up at five a.m. to look perfect when they drop their kids off. They've had a ton of plastic surgery, are fitness fanatics, and never have a hair out of place—and they only invest time in people who look like them. Then there are the 'rah-rah moms'—these ladies look a variety of different ways but are all perky, very involved in the school, and will like you if you help with school activities and are chatty and friendly. Lastly, there is the 'frumpy, dumpy, and lumpys' (she put herself in that category). These are the people who walk around and don't care how they look. They wear whatever clothes are comfortable and enjoy a good hearty meal." She did assure me at the end of our chat that the good news was, whichever category I believed I fell into, there would be people who would want to get to know me because they fell into that category too!

Even if we are able to remain relatively unaffected by these forces and pressures about our personal appearance, we're all familiar with that feeling of sudden panic when somebody—even a family member or close friend—calls unexpectedly to say she's stopping by. Maybe you rush to clean the house, throw all the junk into one room, and shut the door. Maybe you comb your hair and put on some lipstick. Or maybe you search to hide whatever it is you don't want your visitor to see. If you do this because it pleases you and makes you feel good, great! If you do it because you are worried about pleasing "them"—forget it!

I want to turn the whole discussion of appearance upside down. This book is about you—who you want to be and how you would ideally like to feel. What kind of amazing, fully loaded grown-up life are you seeking? If it's all about you, let's focus on what *you* think for a change, rather than what trends, society, and those close to you say and think!

The first question I ask people to consider when discussing their appearance is, what message are you sending to the world?—because you own the power to control this message! Take a moment to think about the question. Let's take a typical day when you are out and about—not at home cleaning the house or dressed up for a special event. Does your appearance say that you're sexually available and might be looking to steal a husband or two? That you're a comfortable, approachable person? That you're tough and not to be messed with, ever? That you're a rebel? A banker? Conservative? Pretty and always smiling? Shy, unsure, and always hiding in the background?

The more important part of this equation is, what do you want the world to see when they look at you? What image do you ideally want to project? What messages are you sending? What are you trying to convey through your appearance? Take a moment to write down the top five messages you want to send to the world and/or the top five words you would like people to use when describing you. Then write down the top five messages that you believe you are sending based on how you usually look. For example, I am: smart, beautiful, confident, together, assertive, in control, conservative, sexy, flirty, approachable, a bombshell, sloppy, casual, rigid and buttoned up, no one to mess with, gentle . . .

Now I'd like you to compare your lists and address any gaps between the two—the messages you want to convey versus the messages you are sending. The most important parts of this equation are, how do I feel about what I am sending out? and how far removed is it from my ideal? If you are dissatisfied or ashamed with the image you're projecting, and the actual and the ideal are completely disconnected, it's time for some hard work on your appearance issues. And that work begins with one rule: *accept the fact that you and only you have control and power over the image that you present to the world.* Facing that reality is a very good beginning.

If you are overweight, it is 100 percent in your power and your power only to lose weight and keep it off. If you are ashamed when friends or colleagues take a ride in your filthy car, you are capable of keeping it washed and detailed. You are able to pick up your clothes off the floor and live in a clean and organized apartment or home—even if that means having it cleaned by someone else. You are free anytime to buy new clothes, get a makeover, dye your hair, and dress in a new style. You can straighten your messy desk and keep paper piles and clutter in your office under control. The issues that we have the most power over are the areas that cause us the most pain and which we are the most lost about how to fix and change! Absolutely, we all struggle with the baggage that keeps us in the swirl of not making changes in these areas. Once you've acknowledged that these goals are actually within your power to attain, the key is staying focused on becoming the person you want to be. It's about fixing what held you back in the past and refusing to make any more excuses—as we'll discuss in a moment.

There are more books, CDs, and information out there than ever before about makeup, hair, clutter, decorating, dressing stylishly, and, always, always the latest craze for getting into shape and losing weight. As I have said before, *you* are the only person who is around you twenty-four hours a day, seven days a week, year in and year out. You are the only one who is in charge of what you put into your mouth, what you put on your body, where you put your paperwork, and the cleanliness and order of your home, car, and workspace. All of these things are 100 percent in your power.

So why the dismal failure rate? What gets in the way of people's taking charge of their own appearance? It can usually be attributed to one of the following causes:

> **EXCUSES** We've all sometimes fallen into the trap of blaming other people or outside forces for our problems. It's easy and tempting. "My parents and whole family are fat, so I'm fat too." "I could be in good shape too, if I could afford her trainer." "I don't have enough money to buy the right clothes to look the way I want." "I'm too busy to worry about getting my car washed." "My spouse doesn't complain about how I look, so I'm not going to worry about it."
>
> Well, see above. You and only you have control and power over the image you present to the world. In short, no more excuses about your appearance.
>
> **BAD HABITS** It takes a great deal of focus, drive, and concerted effort to go after what you want in life, whether that's losing weight or getting organized—whatever behavior you want to change that goes completely against the grain of how you tend to behave and have always behaved. If you've been overweight your entire life or a

complete slob since you were a kid, yes it's hard to change. It's going to take a tremendous amount of energy and perseverance and time to change that habit. Many people claim that they do not have the time, energy, or reserves to put in that kind of work. In the balance/time management chapter, we will talk more about how to better prioritize. However, as I have counseled people over and over again in my office and on television shows, particularly those focusing on weight loss, if it's important enough to you, and you stay focused and are diligent enough, the power is certainly within you. I will discuss this idea further a little later, but trust me: you can change bad habits!

**FEAR OF FAILURE**   This is rooted in defeatist reasoning that if I actually apply 100 percent effort to lose weight or get organized or look as attractive as I can and it doesn't work and I don't get the rewards I thought would come from changing, I might as well not try at all. Or perhaps you fear failure because you have done the same thing over and over and keep ending up with a bad result: gaining weight, losing it, and then gaining it back again; or hiring an organizing expert only to end up with a huge mess within weeks.

**FATIGUE (to the point of exhaustion)**   For those who struggle with weight issues, the most common appearance concern, most of us feel that we've been engaged in a losing battle our whole lives to diet, lose weight, and look great.

We're tired of trying, sick of failing, and just don't want to do it anymore. We have become so discouraged by repeated attempts to change this aspect of our appearance that we throw our hands in the air and no longer believe it is in our power to control.

**LETTING YOURSELF GO**   The phenomenon of getting comfortable—in harsher words, letting yourself go— happens in any long-term relationship, whether it's a friendship, romance or marriage, or a work situation. Think about the day you showed up for your job interview, and then look at what you have on today, four years into your job. Or what you wore on your first date versus a year into dating. Ruts are comfortable, but letting yourself go is simply evading responsibility.

"I don't know what happened—one day I woke up twenty pounds heavier." "Oh, I've been working here forever, I don't need to dress up every day." These are actually conscious decisions you made somewhere along the way—to eat more late at night; to stop going to the gym every day; or to sleep in later, rush out of the house, and look a little messier all day at work. You made the decision to scale down the way you dress for that date or partner or friend. The fact is that people refuse—for months and years on end—to acknowledge that small daily decisions lead to that moment where they wake up one morning and say, "What happened to me?" Or, in a worse-case scenario for many, their partner asks, "What happened to you?"

If you have let yourself go, it was a conscious choice. You may have ignored the slow and gradual erosion of your weight, looks, house, or upkeep. These issues have to do with prioritizing and focus, which we'll discuss further in the balance and time management chapter. Meanwhile, why not start with one small goal toward improving the appearance issue that bothers you most? Choose something manageable, set a time frame, and commit to it. Hopefully your support group and the positive reinforcement you receive will keep you motivated to continue your journey!

## The Power Is Within You

I have appeared on numerous weight-loss reality TV shows to counsel the contestants. Despite the shows' different setups, what we do with each of them is a perfect model for you to adopt in your approach to adjusting your appearance. The other experts on these shows and I know that at the beginning, whatever bad habits and behaviors people have fallen into, they need our help; they can't seem to lose weight on their own. The whole idea of these shows is to rally the necessary support for the contestants—whether it's for sixty days, eighty days, or a year—and then send them on their way. We tell them what to do and monitor them for a certain amount of time. During that process, we also try to teach them how to do it themselves once the show is over and we are out of their lives.

This dynamic is similar to how I run my practice: I don't want to see my clients for a lifetime, and I'm sure they don't want to see me every week for the rest of their lives! The goal behind these shows and therapy is to empower people with the necessary tools, get them on the right path, and let them go to keep bettering themselves. We give them a head start—but the desire and the success will ultimately come from each person's own personal power. At the end of the show, the therapy, this book—you are on your own to ultimately succeed and do it yourself.

I have come to see that people with appearance issues often fall into one of two broad categories: the unconscious person or the self-conscious person. The unconscious person has challenges and issues but either pretends they are not there or ignores them without even trying to change. That person doesn't put much stock in appearance and would like to think no one else notices or judges appearance either. They may try not to look at or judge others in hopes that no one will look at or judge them. They just want everything regarding appearance to "just go away."

The unconscious person says, "I don't care what people think"—even though he or she really does—or, "If I don't pay attention to my appearance or weight, no one else will either." This person is convinced that both these statements are true.

Self-conscious persons manifest their self-consciousness about their looks in two primary behaviors: flaunting the way they look or attempting to hide the way they look. The person who flaunts it might say, "If I wear bright colors and florals, no one will notice my weight," or, "If I show some cleavage or my well-defined arms, it will take the focus off my large nose or yellow teeth." These people feel like they have tricked others by distraction, and often they have even tricked themselves. Flaunters don't only flaunt by the way they dress, but by their words as well. The verbal flaunter is the overweight person who orders a huge meal and then announces, "I'm already fat, so why not?" and laughs, or the badly dressed person who states, "You invited me to be the token slob," or, "As usual, I'm underdressed (or overdressed)."

The self-conscious hider wears baggy clothes, a hat over her eyes, or so much makeup that her face is covered and coated. The self-conscious hider hopes no one will see what she is hiding—she is often even trying to hide from herself! She's always messing with her hair or pulling at her shirt. She's thinking, *If I sit in the corner, wear this baggy shirt or jacket, and keep quiet, I'll just fade into the woodwork.*

I would like you to become a "conscious person," aware and thoughtful about who you are, who you want to be, and who you hope to become. A conscious person takes personal inventory on a regular basis. So let's take a look at how you're feeling right now.

Take a complete body inventory; list what you like about your appearance in one column and what you dislike in another.

In the "Deal or No Deal" chapter, we talked about working with the hand you were dealt in life. We are born with many things that are either difficult or impossible to change: our height, our eye color, our race, our tendency to baldness, a slow metabolism, big hips, thin hair, bad teeth. All of these things came by the genetic roll of the dice; it's what you inherited from your parents. Now, some of these can be addressed—through braces, working out, plastic surgery, and so on—and some cannot.

Height, or the fact that you come from a family where all the women have big hips or small eyes, cannot be controlled. Many other factors can be controlled: your weight, your fitness, your level of grooming. As I mentioned, the great irony is that everyone complains the most loudly about the things they can control—most especially weight. Real grown ups take charge of the issues they can control. They've accepted what they can't change, but they do take charge of their health, the food they put in their mouths, the substances they ingest, the exercise they do (or choose not to do), and their clothing. As a grown up, you're in charge.

## My Plan

The world has set it up that we are constantly critiquing, judging, and often hating ourselves for not measuring up when it comes to our appearance. We need to silence that inner voice. It's no fun to be around a person who's critiquing and judging and hating you all the time—and that person most definitely shouldn't be you! How can you possibly ever feel happy and satisfied if this harsh critic is who you're spending all your time with?

It's time to put the bat down and stop beating yourself up about your appearance. Instead, spend that time figuring out how you want to look as a manifestation of the person you want to be and the image you want to send out to the world, and then show the world that image.

That being said, many people get up, go to work, and attend to their social obligations, but don't put much thought into ownership of their appearance and surroundings. Or taking that a step further, they claim they don't care how they look—and it shows. If you choose to opt out of the appearance game and be sloppy, poorly groomed, and with an office that's a continual mess, then you need to *face the consequences* that your boss may not want to keep you around or send you to an important meeting. Your children might be ashamed of your appearance, and your friends might not invite you to their fancier parties.

If you are single and refuse to put effort into personal grooming, weight management, and exercise, then face the fact that the dating world could be much harder on you. Although there are those who will appreciate the beauty you have on the inside (and they should), many will pass by the opportunity to find out who you really are, because they are not initially attracted by your appearance. In turn, if people are calling you fat or making rude remarks or overlooking your fabulous wit and personality because they don't like what's on the outside, yes, they are inexcusably rude. But you need to take responsibility for the fact that you are choosing to walk around in public looking the way you do, and looking how you look opens the door for people to react however they see fit! Absolutely, no matter how others behave, I want you to be kind to yourself, but that doesn't mean abdicating personal responsibility—a hallmark of the true grown up!

*Use your strengths.* Ask yourself: In what areas of my life—family, children, work—do I take charge and ownership for my own behavior and results? Where am I successful? There has to be one area where the tools for success are working; you simply need to transfer them to the area of appearance to become more of the physical manifestation of what you want to be!

Leaning on members of your support system is crucial when it comes to an endeavor like losing weight. They help you and cheer you along as you learn and practice and internalize the new tools and tricks for your new lifestyle. Leaning on them is a positive step.

But as I cautioned in the support-system chapter, they cannot run your life. No one can do it for you—not your dietician, your nutritionist, your trainer, your workout partner, your housecleaner, your spouse, or your assistant. None of these people, no matter how much they want you to succeed or how much they want to help, are going to do the work for you! You can access all these people for support, but you cannot relinquish control to them, because you need to take control for yourself.

Stop handing over your desire for weight loss to the latest diet book or fitness craze or eating program! I have many friends who are brilliant experts in these fields, and they have individual approaches, but I am sure they would agree with me that in the end they are merely part of your support system. By all means, buy a book or see an expert—that's a smart use of your support system. But if you are someone who buys every new diet book, joins a different gym every few months, or changes your style every couple of months according to what you see on television, then you are not a real grown up. It isn't about utilizing unlimited support; the problem is that you are not sticking to the basics that will get you to where you need to go or you are falling back into previous self-sabotaging behavior and excuses. All the books in the world won't give you focus, determination, or drive. By all means get some help and expert guidance. If you need to latch onto a certain diet program or fitness regimen to get you started, I highly encourage that. But don't constantly hand over the responsibility to some new fad!

I believe that everyone is entitled to have days off from an appearance regime. It's okay to have a day or many days where you don't shower or put on makeup or comb your hair and spend all day in old stained sweatpants. You don't have to worry whether or not you're clean, your house is a mess, your clothes are sloppy—everyone needs a break where they don't have to think about maintenance. You can roll out of bed and allow yourself to forget about it.

But be warned, you are making a conscious decision to be a mess! It's a deliberate adult decision to say, "I am taking the day off. I am going out without showering or brushing my hair, and I'm wearing a baseball cap to the market. I am fully aware that if I run into somebody, I have made that choice to deal with whatever consequences arise from the fact that I am out in public looking like a mess." Similarly, real grown ups know how to make the extra effort to put on their game when necessary. If you are appearing in court or hoping for a discount or meeting people for the first time, part of taking the power and responsibility for yourself is looking the best you possibly can that day.

I spoke earlier about letting yourself go. I personally used to have the bad habit over holiday vacations of saying, "It's the holidays, so I'm not going to think about what I eat." Lo and behold, I could easily put on seven pounds in a week. Now, I may have gained seven pounds in seven days, but to lose those seven pounds? That was a two-month ordeal. One day I had to ask myself, *Why do*

*I allow myself to completely let go? Why do I not say to myself, "I'm going to let myself go just at this party," or, "I'll eat whatever I want this weekend." Why did I allow myself to go hog wild for seven days?* A let-yourself-go hour—great! A let-yourself-go party? Great! A let-yourself-go season? No!

I want you to live consciously, aware of what you are doing every day! If you can do this, you will never wake up one day surprised that you're forty pounds heavier! You are going to wake up at the same place or an even better place than you were five years before!

*Take a compliment.* While you are out living the life you want and becoming the person you want to be, people are bound at some point to compliment you. "I like your shirt." "You look very nice today." "That's a great car." "What a gorgeous home." "You're looking very fit!" Many people—especially those with appearance issues or baggage—become so uncomfortable with any kind of praise that they don't know how to respond. When somebody compliments you on something, whether or not you believe it to be true, you can say thank you—and let the compliment resonate in your spirit. Take it as great feedback that what you're doing is pleasing and noticeable to other people. And accepting a compliment graciously makes the person who gave it to you feel good too!

I am challenging you right now to take your power back! I want you to turn the page to the next chapter all fired up, believing: "I have the power over my own appearance. I am in charge of my image, how I look, and the way the world sees me!

The responsibility lies squarely on your shoulders, and the power is absolutely within you, to change your appearance. If you decide that you are responsible and in control of your own life, you will do it. I have seen amazing transformations . . . and I know you, too, are capable of one!

# 7

# Non-Cents:
## Are You Using Your
## Visa to Pay
## Your MasterCard Bill?

**T**he concept of money evokes strong feelings in most of us. Just thinking about our money (or lack of it) can bring us tremendous joy, sadness, fear, or anger. It can cause us to become tense, anxious, depressed, or resentful or even fill us with panic like we've never felt before. There is simply no piece of paper, coin, or any other inanimate object I know of that has the power to bring out such an incredible range of emotional reactions.

As I've discussed in other chapters, your feelings and baggage drive your behaviors. So naturally when it comes to money, the same applies—your emotions and thoughts, both conscious and unconscious, ultimately drive how you earn, save, and spend your money. The good news is that you can learn to identify and process any negative thoughts or feelings and modify your behaviors to avoid suffering potentially frustrating, or even disastrous, consequences. Perhaps you have seen, read about, or known somebody whose life simply went off the rails in the recent economic recession. There were news stories about both bankers and business executives who took their own lives due to the fallout, as well as heartbreaking stories of men and women who killed themselves and their families because they saw no way out of their financial bind. For others, this intense financial desperation drove them to lie, cheat, and even steal—sometimes from their employers, other times from their own parents or children. The helplessness and hopelessness that led to these actions demonstrate how devastating financial stress can be.

Similar feelings of panic and fear can motivate people to take all kinds of less drastic but nonetheless less-than-ideal actions. Some stay in jobs they hate for a lifetime in hopes of achieving financial stability. Others spend much of their lives in marriages they don't want to be in for the sake of feeling financially secure. Some adults stay enmeshed with and financially dependent upon their parents their entire lives. Many men, women, and couples live in a constant state of financial turmoil because they can't let go of the need to "keep up with the Joneses" and live way beyond their means.

Some of my clients and friends have told me that they have moments of feeling like our whole society is conspiring against them in terms of empowering themselves and managing their money like grown ups! Over the past couple of generations money has become nearly a "virtual" concept. Most of us rarely handle cash, and we conduct the majority of our financial affairs online. Money doesn't exist for most of us in a concrete, tangible form as cash hidden under the mattress did years ago. This distancing ourselves from actually handing over cash for products or services has made the entire subject much easier to ignore.

Our personal finances is the one topic many of us would prefer not to think about, so that's exactly what we do—we don't think about it; many of us do our best to avoid it altogether. The convenience of ATMs, debit cards, online banking and investing, and credit cards is great in terms of saving time and efficiency. The downside is that it is now easier than ever to stick our heads in the sand. How many times have you not known how much you have in your account or forgotten what you charged or how much you spent this month? Have you ever reached in your wallet and wondered where all of your cash has gone? After all, didn't you just withdraw $100 from the ATM? Worse yet, haven't you ever wondered where your paycheck got spent?

For most of us, it's not a subject we discuss either, because talking about how much we earn, spend, save, and lose is often taboo among relatives and close friends, and even between spouses. People who have no problem airing every bit of dirty laundry about their disappointing children, what's happening in the bedroom, a fight with their spouses, and how much they hate their bosses clam up when it comes to talking about money. Most people wouldn't dream of telling even their closest confidante that they are deeply in debt, facing foreclosure, or spending their savings. Why is there such shame and secrecy surrounding this topic?

The reality is that as adults, we are expected to somehow know how to handle money. Many adults are reluctant to admit that they don't know what they're doing or are over their heads, especially when everybody else appears to be managing just fine. No one likes to be judged and found to be unknowledgeable, and many people might question you or think less of you if you admit to being in dire financial straits. It can be humiliating to say that you're in over your head or you're thousands of dollars in debt. It almost implies that you're out of control and unable to take charge of your own life. That debilitating feeling of shame, which we'll speak more about later, often keeps even the strongest of us from admitting to anyone, even our closest friends, that when it comes to money, we have issues.

If any of this sounds like you, I'm here to encourage you to embrace the idea of taking your power back! If you are reading this book, you have acknowledged that you are willing to address the issues that are standing in the way of your becoming a fully loaded grown up and make some changes now! In this chapter we are not going to go over specific strategies on how to find a higher-paying job, manage money and investments, or get out of debt. There are a number of great books and experts with sound advice for every style out there. What I'd like to examine is how you personally feel about money and the psychological underpinnings of these feelings. How much are these hidden forces affecting your overall quality of life?

Let's talk about you and your current financial situation, because, remember, the path to being a fully loaded grown up starts with you assessing you! Are you in a not-so-good place financially? Are you receiving phone calls seeking payments, accruing late fees and finance charges, and looking for lower-interest credit cards to pay off the cards that you already have? Do you let unopened bills stack up? Do you have a place where you keep your bills and check-book, or are you always tearing your house or office apart looking for them at the last minute? Do you borrow from friends and family or owe them lots of money? Do you run out of money or just squeak by before payday? Do you feel like you are forever struggling to catch up, much less keep up? Have you gotten yourself into a financial jam? Do you feel like you never have time to manage your finances, balance your checkbook, pay your bills?

Maybe your financial situation arose from other life circumstances. It may be that you were doing fine financially until a bitter unwanted divorce. You may have put every dime into opening your own business and it didn't survive. You may have accepted having money troubles as part of your quest to seek out your dream of writing or acting for a living and never got that one break. You may have been the victim of the recent economic meltdown. If one or more of these happened to you, the first thing you must do is take some time to grieve. Allowing yourself to experience your feelings after an unpleasant event is not only healing but will allow you to release the pain, regain your strength, and get energy back to move forward.

It is to be expected that you would feel angry, sad, scared, or hurt after trying to make a go of something and having it turn out unsuccessfully. I encourage you to grab a box of tissues, sit down in the middle of the floor, and cry as long as you need to. Or pick up that pillow off your bed and beat on it until you release whatever anger or frustration you are feeling. Scream, yell, cry, complain, spend a couple of days with your head under the covers. Let yourself wallow in your disappointment—you are entitled to it. There is no easy way around it—it stinks when you do the right thing and the wrong result still occurs!

Additionally, I want to make it clear to you that it is okay to fail financially—and that failure can be a temporary state! You will feel better having given your marriage or a business venture or dream a try rather than never giving it a shot at all. After all, you can't win unless you play. It doesn't matter why you've failed to get a grip on your money issues, or whether they're recent setbacks or the result of long-standing bad habits. Rebuilding is done all the time by huge companies, mom and pop businesses, wealthy individuals, and people who are just barely scraping by. You don't need a college degree, a job, wealthy relatives, or even a savings account to begin to create—or re-create—financial stability and security. As a matter of fact, you were born equipped with exactly what you need to begin—and that is *you*!

## The Money/Anxiety Continuum

Really, it all comes down to these questions: How important is money to your dreams and desires? How large a role does money play in achieving those desires? What matters most to you? Are you fine with having a small, modest apartment to live in as long as you are free to travel, raise your children, or do whatever is most important to you? Do you want to surf all the time and don't care at all about a savings account or even a checking account as long as you are near the ocean? Or is it absolutely critical for you to live in an exclusive neighborhood and wear the very latest designer clothes? Are you willing to marry for money or put up with a job you hate with long hours to enjoy the financial rewards and status that come from that income? Whatever you want out of life, this is the goal: managing to support your own preferred lifestyle with a minimum of anxiety.

Imagine that everyone's feelings about money run on a continuum—let's say that at one end, 1, you're feeling absolutely stress free, confident, and financially secure. This could be from winning the lottery, inheriting a great deal of money, or having a secure, high-paying job or business and savings. At the other end, 10 equals pure fear and panic about your financial circumstances. This would include any situation where there is a shortage of money for what you need or want. It might be as dire as: "I can't pay my bills." "I don't know where the rent or mortgage payment will come from." "I can't feed my family or put gas in my car." Others find it stressful when they can cover their basic needs but can't afford any luxuries or extras they want.

It's important to note that your 10 is not somebody else's 10. This scale reflects your individual level of anxiety about whatever your individual circumstances may be. You might be at the top of the anxiety continuum because you can't make your car or house payment, while your friend might consider himself at the top of the scale because he has to cancel that yearly trip to Tahiti. For simplicity's sake, I'm going to group the numbers into three main categories:

- **GREEN LIGHT (Anxiety levels 1–3):** Smooth sailing. I feel relaxed when I think about my financial situation. I have all the material objects that I desire. My income is secure. I have a clear sense of what's coming in and what's going out. I have a plan in place in case of catastrophe. I am on top of any debts and obligations. Financial issues do not disturb my peace of mind. In this state, real grown ups are relaxed, enjoying their financial situations, and continuing to act in ways that will ensure success in the future.

- **YELLOW LIGHT (Anxiety levels 4–7):** Caution advised. This is the most common zone. Thinking about money stresses me out. I prefer not to dwell on my financial situation. I don't have enough to buy that car/house/dress I really want. I'm not good at managing my money. Worrying about money affects my mood. How am I ever going to stop just getting by and get ahead? I'm doing okay but want much more. At this point real grown ups are making plans to reduce their stress; they don't want problems to escalate. They zero in on the trouble spots and take action.

- **RED LIGHT (Anxiety level 8–off the charts):** STOP! This is when financial issues are causing serious problems in every area of your life. I'm so far in debt, I think I'll never get out. I lost my job and can't find a new one. I've gone through a financial catastrophe. I can't pay my bills or support my family. My health is greatly affected by my financial worries; i.e., I can't sleep or eat because I'm so worried about money. I'm irritable, depressed, and considering taking desperate action. When caught in this red zone, real grown ups gather all their resources to attack the problem. They will do whatever it takes to reduce this level back down to something manageable.

The yellow zone represents what I would characterize as the general, free-floating anxiety each of us feels about our personal financial situation. Free-floating anxiety can exist in any area, but it can be particularly impactful when it comes to finances. It is where most adults dwell throughout their lives, because the vast majority of people, even when they have decent enough jobs and some money-management skills, tend to worry about money. Because money is so critical to our lives and disaster can strike at any minute, a certain level of anxiety is inevitable. Our goal is to reduce that feeling to a manageable degree that won't impede your progress and mood in any harmful way—to a steady 3 or 4. In order to do that, let's examine the roots of your individual trouble spots with money.

## Where It Began

Your particular relationship with money and the accompanying stress level arises from several places: your childhood experience, the baggage you've accumulated, and any skills and habits (both good and bad) you picked up along the way. Let's talk about childhood first.

As young children, we weren't aware of what money actually represented. We knew that we wanted certain things—a toy, video game, outfit, candy—and we knew that it felt good when we got them, and we pouted and maybe even cried in disappointment when we couldn't have them. The concept of cost was beyond our comprehension. We had no understanding that leaving lights and water on cost money, or that a Ferrari cost more than a Volkswagen Beetle.

Little kids tend to believe that there is endless money to withdraw at the bank, that a handful of coins can buy a car or help get their parents out of debt, or that the five dollars they made selling lemonade is "a lot of money"—never mind the fact that their parents spent four dollars on cups, lemons, sugar, and the "free" cookies that were given as a bonus to each customer. I can remember when my daughter was five, we knew a lovely woman who lived over a little market in a tiny space on a noisy street. My daughter adored this woman and told me that when her piggy bank was full, she wanted to buy her "a whole house on a quiet street." It will be no surprise to you that my daughter did not understand why she didn't have enough money to do that.

In grade school kids start to learn about dollars and cents in math class. They are tested on which coin is which size, what president is on each bill, and how many nickels make a quarter. They are given problems to solve like: how many $.25 pencils can you buy with $3? or how many hotdogs can you buy for your friends at a baseball game if each costs $1.50 and you have $10 in your pocket? During these years children also become aware that some classmates have certain toys or clothes they want too, and at some point children might have to be told, either directly or in more subtle ways, that some things are too expensive or that their parents can't afford them. It's rare for kids to be included in discussions on how much their parents paid for a house or a car or even a baseball or toy they want. Many parents believe children have no need to know these details and shield their kids, mostly so they won't worry. No matter how it is handled, many kids soon absorb the idea, either consciously or unconsciously, that money is an uncomfortable subject.

However much or little a family has, the grade-school years tend to bring the dawning of awareness of the value of money and the concept that some people have more than others. What's missing is any understanding of how to manage, prioritize, and balance the money we have or will someday earn and spend as adults. Let's talk about the transition from child to fully loaded grown up in terms of your money.

Every family is unique, but let's consider two extremes on the spectrum of parenting styles with regard to monetary support for their children. On one end are the parents who take a completely hands-off approach. Their attitude is that they will support a child until a certain age, say, eighteen or twenty-one, or through high school, college, or trade-school graduation. At that point it's hands off, sink or swim. It's time for the child to join the military, get a job, or find a way to pay for higher education—whatever he or she can manage alone. These children are now in charge of supporting, housing, and feeding themselves. On the other end of the spectrum are the parents who have had a college fund in place since the day their child was born. They assume all educational expenses, as well as spending money, funding a first apartment, a down payment on a first home, even a new car when needed. It is a given that they are always there to financially support their child, no matter how old. Again, most of us fall somewhere between these two examples. But let's examine for a moment the pros and cons of being raised at these extremes and how they affect you psychologically.

Let's say you were essentially on your own at a young age—whether that's because your parents simply didn't have any extra money to help you, or their attitude was that it was for your own good that you learn to take care of yourself financially. You feel such a sense of deprivation, fear, and envy when looking at others who are handed money all the time that you are driven to work hard. You know from an early age that you must rely on yourself as there's nothing to fall back on, and this fear drives you to do whatever it takes to earn money. This might mean finding three jobs, working your way through college, foregoing any luxuries, and quickly learning to save and invest money. You can't wait to become financially secure; it is the driving force in your life.

On the flip side, if this was your situation, you might have felt helpless and defeated before you ever began. In the face of the reality that you have very little cushion or financial support from your parents, you essentially give up. The feeling that you have no one to rely on but yourself brings on overwhelming fear. You might take whatever job you can find and gripe about it and your low pay—maybe for a lifetime. Or you might frantically seek out whoever you can find to support you and do whatever it takes to keep that support coming. You have zero expectations or hopes of raising your financial prospects. You are not motivated, and you feel powerless—fertile ground for chronic depression, anxiety, and even addictions, which we will talk more about later in the book.

Many people think that the ideal parents are those who say and demonstrate: "Financially, I'm always here." When all turns out well, those who are raised this way are motivated to continue down this path and repeat the pattern in their own lives. As adults, these people also want to provide everything for their own children, send them to college, and be able to help them if they need it. They are willing to work to continue the lifestyle they have enjoyed so far. They are motivated and inspired and driven to accomplish—both to please themselves and, often, to please the family that has given them so much.

The downside can be that some of these parents make this seemingly grand and generous gesture in order to control their children, meddle in their lives, or influence their decisions. I have met several adults who have become so intertwined with their parents due to financial ties that they feel they cannot make a decision without parental consultation. Even about what new job to take or who to marry!

Another downside is a phenomenon seen frequently in the children of celebrities and very wealthy families. Often times these people don't learn money handling or money management. They don't have a realistic or healthy relationship with money. They have been raised with so much that they can't ever imagine a lack. There's no correlation between what they contribute and how much money they have. Should something happen to the source of their family income, they might be left floundering, unable to know how to make money, much less manage it. They've never needed to know how to survive on their own.

As always, the goal is to strive for balance. This means a balanced relationship between you, your money, and all those who are associated with it.

## Financial Baggage

This book is all about empowering you, so I'd like to talk for a moment about how baggage can keep you from becoming a conscientious, aware money manager in charge of your own financial fate. The experiences we have throughout life, particularly early on, impact our every thought, feeling, and behavior for years to come. Whatever emotional baggage you are carrying concerning money can be a very damaging burden if you haven't properly processed the harmful events and resulting emotions. If you intellectually know the right things to do in terms of managing your money, then why aren't you doing them? Is your baggage causing you to behave in ways that are not in your own best financial interest?

The truth is that money is merely a symbol. For many of us, what money equals is power—or lack of. If you are a person who equates money with power, you probably use what you have to buy what you want or to hire people to do what you want them to do—in other words, to control them. That's a great, strong position to be in. But let's examine the other side of the fence, where most of us live. Most of us are dependent in terms of the power equation regarding money—your boss won't give you a raise, your spouse is the breadwinner, you've lost your job, your parents still support you. Hopefully whoever holds financial power over you is benevolent and treats you fairly and respectfully. If they don't, you probably feel helpless, trapped, and impotent.

In terms of empowering yourself, I have found that there are two underlying issues that trip up many people when it comes to their finances: low self-esteem/self-confidence and trust. Some people go through life never feeling particularly great about themselves. They suffer from low self-confidence—either by temperament or because they have taken more than their fair share of hits. Family problems, work or appearance issues, illness, or a string of difficult relationships may have taken their toll. Any of these make life difficult enough, but when money enters into this equation, as it must, people with low self-confidence need to be more diligent than most, as lack of self-esteem and self-worth will most likely play out in terms of their finances.

These negative feelings might drive such beliefs as: You don't deserve more than you grew up with. Not getting what you want is your lot in life. You're not good enough or smart enough to earn a lot of money, marry somebody who does, or have friends who are successful. Such beliefs could leave you completely dependent on somebody else to either support you or make all of your financial decisions, even with the money you earn. This is behavior I see more frequently in women, who tend to have a much harder time than men in speaking up at work, negotiating pay and raises, and standing up for themselves in financial discussions with spouses and family members.

A more positive outcome, given these feelings of low self-worth, is that some people are able to channel and use them to drive themselves to achieve. Their uncomfortable feelings spur them on to financial success. Those who end up retreating or remaining passive instead of moving forward tend to have weaker support systems, less inner drive and resilience, and weaker passion and desire.

The best advice I can give concerning money and low self-confidence is: move forward anyway. Confidence is built by taking action and achieving success, so you need to start by building small successes. Whether it's taking one class, balancing your checkbook, or cleaning up your credit report, these are all good steps.

Trust is the other area I'd like to discuss in terms of baggage surrounding money. There are several layers of trust as it concerns your finances. First and most important, *you*: Do you have trust in your own ability to earn money, manage it, and control spending it? Second, your circle: can you trust your parents to leave an inheritance? Can you trust your friends to pay you back if you loan them money? Can you trust your boss or company to have the money to meet payroll every time? Can you trust your company to run efficiently enough to stay in business? Can you trust your spouse to support you and provide for you if you are a stay-at-home parent?

Finally, the outsiders: can you trust those professionals to whom you entrust your money? Is the person you rely on for financial advice completely above reproach? What about your accountant, real estate agent, stockbroker? These days, can you even trust that the money in your bank will be safe?

If your anxiety level concerning money is in the red zone, you might wish to examine whether past trust issues are affecting you adversely today. You may have been betrayed by a friend or family member at some point. You may have been swindled in business. You may have grown up with parents who controlled you financially, or you may have had romantic relationships in which others abused your finances or depended on you completely to support them. It's time to think clearly about whether or not there is real evidence concerning any persons or situations that are causing you anxiety about your money now.

One builds trust by first building up trust in oneself, which starts by building a solid foundation. Next, you must pay attention to any warning signs. If someone has been trustworthy for years, then you might assume he will be trustworthy moving forward. Finally, when it comes to that third level, you want to go to someone who has a great reputation and was recommended by someone whose advice you trust.

## Seven Bad Habits

Remember when I said that we learn what we live? Our childhoods and baggage can cause us to act in ways that do not serve us well in terms of our money. See if you recognize yourself in any of these seven common behaviors:

- A common attitude I see is the bury-your-head-in-the-sand approach to money. This is the willful avoidance of all money matters, manifesting in everything from refusing to open bank statements, to letting bills pile up, carelessly spending money, buying recklessly and deciding to worry about it "later." This attitude is rooted in fear—fear of taking responsibility for your own financial situation or fear of facing bad news that could emotionally overwhelm you.

- Filling-the-hole phenomenon. I feel alone, unwanted, unfulfilled. I don't have a romantic relationship, so I'll at least have designer clothes or a beautiful couch or . . . I don't have any close friends to confide in, so I'll buy things online that I don't really need. I feel empty inside, and I will feel alive by shopping, spending money, and living way beyond my means. This behavior is rooted in sorrow and a feeling of lack. Spending money temporarily fills the hole but absolutely does not fill the lack that led to the hole.

- Using money as a weapon. The rebellious spender is somebody who is driven by anger. She might spend to get back at a parent or spouse. She might be angry with herself for not performing well enough and spend money or shop to soothe her irritation. These types of people also control others through money—the parents who finance their children, then tell them how to live; the spouse who demands certain things from a stay-at-home partner, etc.

- Need to impress. These people go heedlessly into great debt in order to live way beyond their means—with cars, houses, vacations, and other status symbols completely out of proportion to their income. As a friend of mine once said, "Where I come from, we call them $30,000 millionaires." This behavior is rooted in insecurity and shame. People who engage in this don't feel good enough, so they buy a car or house they can't afford to impress others. They might give lavish gifts or cater fabulous parties for others in an attempt to buy goodwill or friendship. This is a false building of self-esteem. These persons feel that material items make them better and more desirable, when inside they have not changed at all.

- Laziness/habituation. Maybe you were raised with plenty or had a lucrative job or a wealthy partner, and you became accustomed to a certain level of spending. Then you refuse to change your behavior when your financial situation changes. You may find spending lavishly an impossible habit to break. Be aware that it may eventually lead to a full-blown shopping addiction. A sense of entitlement is driving this behavior. I've always had this, I should have this, I deserve this, so I'm getting it now and not worrying about the cost.

- Penny-pinching. This is generally driven by fear and lack of trust. These people may have endured deprivation when they were young or grew up in poverty or suffered a great financial loss in life. Now they make everybody else's life miserable with their stinginess. This group may also include those who have worked hard for their money and have such a fear of losing it that they hold on irrationally tight to every last cent.

- Digging the hole a little deeper. I'm already so far down, why not go deeper? Driven by helplessness, feeling a lack of power, and angry, these people know they are already in debt and are worried about their money situation but basically throw their hands in the air and say so what. It's so bad, how can it get worse? Head-in-the-sand people refuse to even acknowledge their money issues or the extent of their debt; they are so frightened they stay away. The digging-the-hole person reacts by saying, so what, I'll just file bankruptcy if it comes to that.

As you read over this list of behaviors and what drives them, you may recognize yourself in many categories. You may exhibit elements of all these behaviors when it comes to how you handle money, which is why it's so important to become aware of what is driving you. It's crucial to know who you are and what you want, need, and expect in terms of money. As your desires and circumstances grow and evolve over your lifetime, so will your reactions and responses.

## Moving Ahead

Fully loaded grown ups have mastered a set of skills to keep their finances and their emotions on an even keel.

- **REALITY.** If you dropped out of high school, it will be harder for you to achieve the income of an attorney. If you earned advanced degrees, there will be more high-paying job opportunities available to you. Real grown ups take a serious look at their qualifications and skill sets and live in reality in terms of how they're going to earn their living.

- **RECOVERY.** If your childhood experiences and baggage are at the root of your financial issues, it's time to seek professional help in terms of therapy.

  If and when they face a financial meltdown, real grown ups realize they will need to fight and work hard to fix the problem. Fortunately, they have the strength and tools to do so!

- **PREVENTION.** This means being constantly aware of the state of your finances and consistently making plans and adjusting them as circumstances change. Always have a backup plan for if and when the worst should happen. Keep your anxiety level in the green zone—and if it starts to rise, deal with it immediately!

- **EDUCATION.** This means taking responsibility for keeping up with the information you need to manage your own finances—whether that's understanding your credit-card terms or handling sophisticated investments. For those who like to read, the shelves are packed with best sellers about every aspect of money. The most important part is finding a technique that works for you. Do your research, check out a few books from the library, and choose the author whose approach most appeals to you. For those who prefer meetings, workshops, and seminars, the same applies.

- **SUPPORT.** Real grown ups reach out for support—whether that's getting advice from a friend, going to a 12-step group, or hiring a credit counselor. If managing money is your weak spot, then commit to finding the right person or company to manage your money for you. The caveat is, of course, that you oversee what they're doing and stay informed, not just hand over the responsibility to someone else!

Finally, please keep in mind that money will always be an uncomfortable topic in our society. You must learn to tolerate that discomfort, because it's unavoidable. You have to pay your bills no matter what. You have to file taxes every year no matter what. For once, logic must override your emotion—this is left-brain material. Dollars and cents. Plus and minus. Plain and simple, your emotions and baggage cannot get in the way of math! Real grown ups learn to separate emotion from money and handle their finances in the most logical, methodical, and reliable way possible so that they're free to enjoy their lives however they choose!

**8**

# Job: Got One?
# Like It?

**A**s children, we were inspired and excited about the prospect of someday becoming a firefighter, a nurse, a doctor, a teacher, a wrestler, a hairdresser—you name it, we wanted to do it. We put on costumes and role-play anything and everything our imaginations allowed—free of any self-doubt, criticism, or judgment. Maybe you walked around town wearing a firefighter hat, a tutu, or a superhero cape—didn't many of us hope to be one of those too, fighting evildoers and rescuing those in need? Maybe you gave your babysitter a manicure or played doctor and listened to your friend's heart with a plastic stethoscope. Or perhaps you played chef, serving pretend food in red and yellow play cookware, asking your diners if they wanted more. Whatever you did to play out job fantasies, I am sure you were happy and took great pleasure in imagining your future.

Then you started to get older. You learned the truth about what your parents and loved ones thought you should do, what your skill set was, and what would actually make you the living you would need to survive or maintain a desired lifestyle. Translation: you grew up, and reality collided with your vision of what you once dreamed you could become.

Your job, or career, is about so much more than a paycheck or the use of your skills. It is an integral part of who you are and impacts your identity and the way you think, feel, and behave. Have you ever noticed that "What do you do?" is generally the first question people ask when they meet you? They ask this to connect, make conversation, and learn more about the person they just met, you. Your answer sets the tone for how they view you and eventually how they will react to you and judge you. Your response dictates what they will think your income level is, how educated you are, the kind of car you drive and the place you live, whether you're a hard worker or not . . . It isn't just a job. This is the one category above everything else that identifies you to the people you meet.

You can separate yourself from your friends. You can clearly distinguish yourself from your mate, no matter how much you love him or her or how close the two of you are. You can disown your family or move thousands of miles away. But you cannot separate yourself from your work—for good or for bad, it represents you and defines you—not to mention supports you!

Let me say at the outset, because I feel strongly about this, that what I'm going to cover here is not just directed at people who work outside of the home. There are all kinds of scenarios that are very real jobs—the kinds that are difficult to perform and can be difficult to get away from. Where you don't punch a time clock, your hours never seem to end, you don't earn a paycheck, and you rarely get a day off. Whether you are raising children, caring for others, or have simply divided responsibilities with a mate so that you are the person who stays home, everything we talk about in this chapter will still apply. It doesn't matter if you have a huge staff and impressive title or you are chasing a three-year-old all day. It doesn't matter if you telecommute or have an executive office downtown. It's not even about the money—though of course that is a main consideration for many of us!

It's about the meaning you find in whatever work you are doing and the contribution you are making to society, however you choose to define that. This goes to the heart of who you are and can impact every other category we talk about in this book. It's a given that your work usually governs your finances. Your work will most certainly impact your intimate relationships and support system—if you're moody, irritable, and whining about work all the time, people will eventually grow tired of hearing these complaints or simply want to avoid being around you. Time management is greatly affected—primarily because most of us spend the biggest chunk of our waking hours at our jobs, and most of us work for the vast majority of our lives. Not to mention how much time it's possible to waste sitting at your desk staring into space, thinking about how much you hate your boss, playing on the Internet or talking on the phone instead of doing what you are supposed to be doing, or taking the longest breaks and lunch hours you can. Flexibility plays a huge role in your job arena—consider that most people today have more than one career in their lives. Some have four or five! And if you are a stay-at-home parent, flexibility in the job of child rearing is a must! Apart from love and intimate relationships, which we discussed in an earlier chapter, there is simply no greater force in your life than what you choose to do and how you do it each day— what most of us call a job.

## What Drives You at Work

When you look at your career as a whole, including where you are today, what you hope to accomplish, and what might be holding you back, it's crucial to talk about drive. Drive is the key motivator that leads us to take the steps to get where we need to go. Driving a car is a perfect metaphor, as it's literally getting you from one place to another preferred destination. If it is your car, you are best off taking the wheel in order to assure that the vehicle goes where you want it to go and that it is driven safely. You must take charge of driving your life in the same way.

Some people have their innate drive nurtured and enhanced; others are naturally predisposed to having strong wills and the determination to succeed. Some men and women just seem born to greatness. Whatever the amount of drive you possess, it began with your childhood, so let's go back for a moment and talk about the roots of drive.

All children come into this world wanting and needing specific things. No matter where they live, their socioeconomic class, or who is raising them, it starts with the basics: the need to be warm, fed, and dry. As babies begin to become aware of their surroundings, they start to point at the things they want. They point at a bottle, a blanket, a pacifier, even Mommy and Daddy. As they grow older, they have better motor skills and begin to reach out for a balloon, a doll, a truck, or a loved one. When they don't get what they want, they may cry or whine and even throw a fit that could bring down a house. These desires and those dramatic responses are innate parts of a normal child's development. Although they can be irritating to those around them, they are the beginning of their lifelong pursuit to go after what they want.

As we mentioned in the chapter on dynamic communication, children quickly begin to take their cues from their caregivers' behavior and how responsive they are to their desires. Some of us learn that if we turn our drive on full-bore to pursue the desired object, we will eventually succeed in getting what we want. When things that we want or need are consistently withheld from us, we begin to react in one of several ways: realize that we have to get what we want by ourselves with no help; retreat, give up and don't ask anymore; or rebel and become aggressive and angry.

At school, spelling bees, pop quizzes, physical fitness tests—any competitive test that pushes children beyond their comfort zones—are strong early indicators of drive. It is easy to recognize the most driven and determined kids, the ones who say, "I'm going to do this no matter what. I'm going to sit here and work and learn and practice until I figure it out." Others say, "I'll never be able to do this; I'll just take the failing grade." Finally, there are those kids who sit and wait and hope that someone will give them the answers. These three broad types of kids turn into three kinds of grown ups with three separate approaches to work challenges.

When you look at your life today as an adult, particularly your job, are you getting the things you need and/or want out of it? Are you the kind of person who, when faced with reaching an academic or professional goal, asks, What am I going to do to get there? What angles will I pursue? What new skills do I need to acquire? Who will help me get this done? Do I need to delegate any of this? If you are considering these questions, then you are taking responsibility for your life and are thinking in the direction of success. Or are you someone who sits back, waits, and hopes that desire will magically come to you and your work will miraculously get done? Or are you a victim, someone who sits and cries and complains, saying, "I'll never have . . . No one will give me . . . I can't make this happen . . . I'm doomed . . ." Or worse yet, are you behaving like the young child we talked about earlier, crying and whining and throwing a temper tantrum because you haven't gotten what you wanted?

Each of these scenarios was likely played out at some point when you were a child—some more frequently than others. If the force of your will and desire made something happen and won you the reward, it reinforced your desire to always keep chasing what you aspire to have. If you sat back while everything was handed to you, it likely taught you to be passive and wait. If nothing was ever just easily given to you, you may have adopted that victim personality that says, "I'll never get that, I'll never be that . . ." and refuses to even try. Finally, maybe you learned to fight harder because you developed a passion to achieve since you were always denied.

When it comes to your job, it is critical to become an action-oriented grown up. This type of adult seeks out and obtains the kind of career and job he or she wants or is working to get. If she doesn't yet have the career or job title she aspires to, she will take whatever job she has to in order to pay her bills while continuing to work toward her desired position. The action-oriented grown up lives with the motto "short-term pain/long-term gain" and says things like, "I need to still cover my expenses while I study to become a nurse . . . or earn my degree . . . or train in computer science," or, "I will do this now, knowing that I am building my skills to do what I want to do later." This person researches the best schools to go to, the kinds of job skills and degrees needed, knows who can advise her, and plays up the skills she already has. She is diligent, networks, researches—in short, does whatever it takes to get hired—or at least gain entry into her field of choice. If she's not yet in the right job, she is building her skills and keeping her eye on the prize. Action-oriented grown ups don't sit around and wait for somebody else to do it for them, or for a company to call them and make an offer, or for a boss to victimize them. They move forward constantly. Movement makes for change and progress.

The roots of action-oriented behavior can spring from negative emotions; it's all about how they are channeled. Many of the most successful businesspeople in the world are motivated by pure fear or anger. Fear that they won't make, have, or do enough; fear that they won't be able to provide for their families; fear of being like their parents; fear of *not* being like their parents; fear of not measuring up; fear of their parents' disapproval. These people harness fear into action with tremendous results and success. Fear can be an incredibly strong driver, and for action-oriented people, it often is. Other action-oriented grown ups are motivated more by anger. They are frustrated that they grew up poor. They're angry that their parents told them to be successful, they should become a doctor or some other professional, not a musician, and they spend a lifetime proving their parents wrong. Or they're furious that a boss treated them badly or someone ripped them off; they think, *I'm going to show him!* and set out to do so.

Then there are those I call the sit-and-wait-and-hope grown ups, men and women who do not take ownership over their career desires and who expect that a job will somehow be handed to them. These people often fall into some sort of job, then coast along for years whether or not they're doing something they like or are suited for. The job chose them, in a sense. If something unexpected happens and they get laid off, these grown ups might call a few people and send out a couple of resumes, but ultimately, they hope somebody will have a need for them, think of them, and call *them*. If that doesn't happen, they hope they will be rescued by somebody else, either offering them a job or wanting to marry them or at least finance their lifestyle. (Of course, there are action-oriented women and men who make it their entire mission to go out and find someone to support them—but that's a whole different subcategory!)

The sit-and-wait-and-hope people are often motivated by fear, laziness, and/or self-consciousness, overwhelmed by the fear of putting themselves out there in the world, or exhausted at the thought of even trying. If they don't try, they won't fail. On the flip side, these people may also be motivated by a sense of entitlement—they feel that everything should be handed to them. They don't understand why a dream job is not theirs, even when they've done absolutely nothing to get it!

Stay-at-home moms and dads sometimes fall into this category in that they believe that having a child means they have "fallen into" the need to stay home. That once was true, but in our current society it is not. In my experience, parents who feel like they do not want to be at home raising children do not do a good job raising them! An unhappy primary caregiver makes for an unhappy home and children. Resentment builds, the children feel like they are being raised by someone who doesn't want to be there all day, and ultimately it even impacts the marital relationship.

Finally, victimized grown ups in a work setting just know the success they desire will never happen, that they're not capable, good enough, or deserving enough—so they settle. They take the first job that comes along or marry the first person who shows any interest and abdicate any responsibility for making a living. Because they don't feel confident about their skills and value, they tend to get trapped in abusive work relationships. These people will automatically accept an environment where they are made to feel bad about themselves and their contributions—it's two puzzle pieces fitting perfectly together. They manage to find the supervisors or partners who are the exact opposite of somebody who believes in them, recognizes their value, and appreciates their potential. Remember, when the people you work for see you as "less than," you have nowhere to go but down.

Just like some very successful businesspeople, victimized grown ups may also be motivated by fear and/or resentment/anger. However, they don't channel these feelings as productively or reap financial rewards. They are too afraid that they'll never become what they want to be or have or get what they should in the work world. They're angry because they feel life has been too hard on them, and they don't want to work anymore. They're tired, they're fed up, no one will ever appreciate them, and they don't want to do the grind for another minute. Those who are victimized can't allow themselves to be happy or productive, because they spend all their time and energy and focus dwelling on being angry and scared instead of focusing on the possibilities in the future. They believe deep in their hearts that people have always treated them badly and always will; it's their lot in life to have dead-end jobs where no one likes them or appreciates their talents and efforts.

Let's say you are one of the people in this last group. You might believe that all your drive in the area of your career was beaten out of you; you have been disappointed too many times, or you never had any drive to start with. The good news is that drive is something you can create on your own. You can manufacture drive. It starts by doing it anyway—the marketing folks at Nike products had it right! Just do it!

*Doing it anyway* means seeking role models in your chosen field who have the innate drive to succeed and modeling your behavior on theirs. Persons who do not have this innate drive must become far more mindful and deliberate. They need to train themselves to be goal oriented. They need to make lists of baby steps to take to get them where they want to go, and work those steps. They need to set monthly, yearly, and lifetime goals. They need to make backup plans. They need friends who are driven and focused on work and success—this means getting yourself involved with the people at work or acquaintances who are motivated to succeed. We discussed this more in the support-system chapter.

## SPONGES VERSUS BRICKS

There's an easy way to divide people in relation to work: there are sponges and there are bricks. Sponges are people who soak up as much information as they possibly can in order to build on who they are, what they can do, and who they know so they can climb their way up the ladder or go on to even greater successes. Employers love these spongy folks because they rightly perceive them to be flexible, open, and willing to evolve and grow. Then there are the brick people. They are not open, because they believe that they already know everything there is to know. Or else they don't want or care to know, because they just want to get home to their television set each night. These people tend to not rise up the ladder and rarely set the world on fire.

If you are not someone who was born with innate drive, you need to make efforts to be a sponge. You need to exert effort and time toward consciously absorbing knowledge, information, guidance, and nurturing. It's best if you can find a mentor or boss who sees your potential and is interested in helping you grow. If you are not open to finding or cultivating that sort of relationship, as we discussed in the chapter about support systems, then you won't easily achieve the benefits that those relationships have to offer.

Remember, this book is about getting what you want, and that means very different things for each person. What are you looking for? What will it take for you to have not just a job you like, but one you love? For some people it's all about the paycheck. Others care more about appreciation, doing good in the world, giving back, status, or any number of other factors. What are your wants and your needs, and how much are you getting of either?

Fully loaded grown ups in the career department are armed with the knowledge of who they are and what kinds of jobs or careers will best suit them. They know what their strengths are and the skills they possess. They are clear about their passions and have either incorporated them into their careers or make time for them outside of the office. They know their own personal preferences— one's a night owl and needs to work in the evenings. Another has family obligations on weekends and finds a job that will never require him to work then. Another is happy taking a job for less money as long as she is eligible for bonuses and sales commissions. They all want to work hard in spurts and sit back when they're financially in good shape.

Which kind of person are you in terms of needs? Let me ask you this: can you see yourself delivering mail on a regular route or having a traditional sit-at-your-desk-day-after-day occupation? Would you ever consider working on commission or in sales? Is your temperament best suited to a structured, predictable job, where you might have the same truck, same route, same houses, or same tasks and duties day after day? Or do you prefer a job where you fly by the seat of your pants, dazzle people with charm, and tolerate fluctuating income each month? Where you have to hustle to make money, make cold calls, take rejection, possibly have your mood regulated by how much money you make (or don't). Can you take risks, connect with people when you meet, convince them to buy what you're selling? Do you like the security of being an employee, or do you long to be your own boss? What would an ideal workday be for you?

Give these questions some thought, so you will be less likely to wind up in a job that doesn't suit your temperament and causes you misery.

## Getting Unstuck

However they wound up in that position, there are a whole lot of people out there who feel trapped and miserable in their jobs. Some get proactive and start to think and plan and strategize on how to get out of the unhappy workplace as soon as possible and do something else or at least make a plan to improve their current situation. There's nothing like having a job or boss you hate and dreading going to work each day to motivate more action-oriented people to either get out or take steps toward adjusting their conditions. The real danger lies in that moment when you begin to get the feeling that you have no options. When you believe that for whatever reason you cannot leave your job, you are wandering into dangerous territory.

Maybe you're in the Golden Handcuff—this is the job that you don't want to maintain but feel trapped into staying with by the benefits and/or perks. It could be that you are too dependent on the income, attached to your coworkers, or feel lucky to have any job at all in a depressed industry. Maybe you're suffering now but feel like you have to stick with it to work your way up the ladder. You must gain experience or a credential. You're putting yourself through school. You fear what your family and friends would say if you left. You take a lot of grief as a customer-service representative because you hope one day to become a manager. Maybe you're doing whatever it takes to put food on the table and feed your family until the economy improves. This is what your father and grandfather did so you have to do it too. You can't leave a family business.

The questions to ask yourself, and answer realistically are these: Is this job for the meantime, or is this forever? Is your belief that you cannot leave valid, or is fear or lack of self-esteem holding you in place? Hopefully you are staying at this place that you so dislike for a greater good. You are enduring some discomfort to get where you need to go, and you realize that if you work hard, do a good job, make a good impression, and are a reliable employee, you will indeed at some point jump to the next level, or you'll get what you need and exit. But what if you are truly stuck in a dead-end job? Let's say there is no jumping. There is no next level or place to go.

No doubt, if this is your situation, you are seeking ways to cope and relieve your stress. The first thing I would say, after establishing that this is truly a "life sentence" situation—is to seek out healthy ways to relieve stress. There are plenty of unhealthy habits that are easy to fall into—like visiting the vending machine, gossiping with coworkers, handling your personal life at your desk, taking frequent cigarette breaks, drinking after work every night . . . anything to distract yourself from a bad situation.

I once had a client who actually got fired because she visited the vending machines a few times too often. The office had installed them for the employees' convenience, but she fell into the habit of giving herself a work break every hour and heading to the vending machines, which were on a different floor, near the lunchroom. She used to leave her desk, go to the machines and buy her item, sit down at a table and eat for seven or eight minutes, then take the elevator back up to her floor. Basically she was taking a ten or fifteen-minute break every hour. She was actually relieved when they fired her, because she was over her head and hated her job but felt trapped and unable to get herself out of the situation. Being fired is not a great outcome—oh, and with all of that vending-machine eating, she gained weight as well.

What I want you to do is avoid a state of depression and battle the concept of feeling stuck. In truth, I believe that there is no such thing as being truly trapped. On some level you are making a choice to be in that situation. What is the reason you are making that choice? Admitting to the fact that you have power over leaving and that you are not truly stuck helps take away the feelings of being trapped and helpless, because you will begin to realize that the power is within you to stay or make a change. There are always other options; you may just be unable to see them right now.

But let's say, for now, you really are stuck—the economy is bad, you have to learn more skills and stay where you are; you have been looking for something else, but it hasn't come along yet. What I want to say to people who need the jobs they've got for now for whatever reason is that high-functioning grown ups will try to maximize their happiness in the jobs they're stuck in. They might focus on the fact that they pay the bills every month and provide for their families. Or that they know they'll never get fired because their employer loves them, or that they have one great friend in the office. They concentrate on whatever benefits they have, whether that's being allowed to leave early some days if their child is sick, or taking advantage of great insurance. The key is appreciating the benefits your job gives to your life, even if the job itself doesn't make you happy.

Remind yourself to keep the bigger picture in mind. What are you actually doing and producing? Maybe you work in a restaurant and you can feel happy that you are serving hungry customers good food with a cheery attitude. Can you realize that as an overwhelmed preschool teacher, you are guiding and influencing young minds? Can you get past hammering nails in the baking hot sun all day to realize that you are creating a home for somebody to live in? What in your job can you pull out and place in the bigger picture about your contribution?

I'd like to address the people who, because of unemployment, may believe that they are contributing nothing. The fact is that even the most qualified and confident people can be thrown into panic and despair by the loss of their jobs through no fault of their own. Once again, we can't discount the luck of the draw. Some people threw a quarter in the slot machine and hit the jackpot. They just walked right into a great job and career and made a windfall. Others worked hard their whole lives for no payoff. In the recent recession, millions of men and women who were behaving responsibly and like grown ups lost their jobs despite performing well. This is why it's so important to always have a backup plan. When it comes to jobs, there is a great deal of uncertainty—not necessarily concerning your own skills and abilities, but concerning your company, your industry, the national economy. All of us need to have a fallback position if something goes wrong tomorrow. Is it that you will go work at a retail store? Will you move home and enter your family business? Will you take your skill set somewhere else? A real grown up actually thinks about these things—all the time—and has a plan in place.

If you truly believe you cannot change your situation and are sinking into a quagmire of despair, then it's time to seek counseling and really lean on your support system to regain your sense of hope and possibility. This is a crisis that needs to be attended to immediately, because you need to get back into the game as soon as possible.

## Satisfaction

The ideal job is one where if you didn't need the money, you would still be happy to do it anyway. The goal to work for is that feeling 75 percent of the time, or four out of five days, or ten months out of the year, where you feel you had a good day, you contributed, and you are generally content with what you put out and got back in return. You're probably not jumping for joy every day about your job, but you feel satisfied at the end of most days.

It's not all about what you're getting back from those around you at work and how much money you made. It's how you feel inside. Do you generally feel satisfied and happy within yourself that you did good work, even if it's unacknowledged and unappreciated? Keep in mind that real grown ups have reasonable expectations about their careers; no job or career will ever be perfect, no matter how great the financial rewards. That's where the idea of "satisfiers" comes in—the majority of the time, these are what keep you feeling good walking out the door each day.

Over the course of my career I spent some time working with large companies in employee relations. What makes people happy at work are what corporate psychologists call "satisfiers." A paycheck is the main motivator that causes people to show up for work day after day, but satisfiers are the intangible elements such as being close to your coworkers, feeling appreciated by your boss, the sense that you are giving back, and your travel or vacation perks. In what you are doing today, how many satisfiers does your job provide? Everybody should be able to name at least three satisfiers in his or her job. If you cannot come up with three things in your career, then you need to take a long hard look at changing your situation.

\* \* \*

**Recently I was out running errands with my kids and we stopped** for a quick lunch. The place wasn't fancy, just your basic chain restaurant. A young man who had recently graduated from college served us, and we chatted a bit. I learned that he was seeking a "real" job in the field he'd received his degree in, but meanwhile he had taken a job as a waiter so he could support himself. This young man was the best waiter I've ever had.

He was polite, accommodating, made sure to give us plenty of extras, and was great with my kids—all without being intrusive. He was so lovely that at the end of the lunch I paid the bill, left a standard gratuity, and as we were walking out, I handed him a twenty-dollar bill. I've never done anything like that before, and I said to him, "You are the nicest, best waiter I've ever had, and I would like to give you something a bit extra because I know you are not yet in the career you want."

He was completely taken aback. "I act like this every day and have for the past six months I've been doing this job, and no one has ever said or done anything like this before. You are the first person who has ever recognized my efforts to go the extra mile and do a good job." This story is not about how I parted with twenty bucks or had a great waiter. The moral of the story is that I had a mediocre meal in a mediocre restaurant and was served by someone who would have much preferred to be doing something different with his life. However, we both left that day feeling great. I was delighted with the service; he felt validated and appreciated. I tell this story only to encourage you to find the motivation to do your best and try your hardest every day—it could lead to a great feeling!

Yes, this book is about you and what you want, but we're all part of a society, and ultimately what you do and how you interact with others while you're doing it can lead to a win/win. And when that happens, you really have won the career game.

---

## THINKING BIG, THINKING SMALL, NOT THINKING AT ALL!

People who think big are fully loaded grown ups! They have a plan, a purpose, and a passion. They are willing to pay their dues because they have their eye on a bigger future. They have found satisfiers that make them happy. They rally their resources to help them succeed. They have a backup plan should things go wrong.

Then there are those who think small. These people are just glad they have a job and a paycheck and a schedule every day. They do the bare minimum of tasks required of them. They aren't interested in improving their job performance as long as they remain employed. They don't volunteer for special projects or take on extra work. They don't cultivate higher-ups in their office or industry. They are most interested in their breaks, lunch hour, and holiday schedule.

Finally there are those who don't think at all. This includes people with no motivation who prefer not to work because whatever job they could get is beneath them. They would rather sit home and do nothing. Somehow, they often manage to find people to enable them in this goal. Now more than ever, people are going back home to live with their parents because they have a sense of entitlement, they have become lazy, they have no work ethic, and they prefer to be supported rather than get out on their own and make a living.

I don't even need to point out that grown ups who want to live fully loaded lives take responsibility for their fate. They seize control of what they do, because they want the best for themselves. They want to be the best mail carrier or oncologist or salesperson they can be!

9

# Gotta Have It!

**A**s tiny babies, we were intensely attached to our mothers' breasts or our bottles in the most powerful way. We quickly became habituated to being nourished on a regular basis. As we grew out of early infancy, many of us were put on a predictable schedule that our caregivers could follow to the letter—when the clock struck three or seven or twelve, the sounds of our needy, demanding cries echoed throughout the house! In addition to satisfying our hunger, this ritual offered comfort and never failed to soothe us. Being breast fed or given a bottle made us feel satiated and connected; not only to our caregiver but also to the object itself.

Some might argue that as babies, we were, in a way, addicted to the breast or bottle, quite apart from the fact that it provided our necessary sustenance. We felt an incredibly strong desire to have it when we wanted it, were anxious when it was delayed, and became stressed and felt helpless when it was denied, crying our eyes out until we received it. Our quick rush of excitement when we were finally granted the object of our desire was followed by the soothing calm of getting what it was we wanted/needed so badly.

No harm came out of our wanting our bottles, having them or soothing ourselves with them. Our families and doctors knew that eventually there would come a day when we would be willing and able to live without them. I cannot tell you how many times I have told anxious parents not to stress out over their child's attachment to the bottle or pacifier—I have yet to see a college student drinking out of a bottle or sucking on a pacifier unless it was for a college costume or gimmick!

Much like a baby craves and yearns for its bottle, pacifier, or favorite blankie, we adults have a similar pull and "need" toward various substances and activities to give us happiness and comfort. It is when these pulls become insatiable needs that interfere with our daily functioning that we have to consider addiction. At this moment, none of this may resonate with you personally; however, I suggest you read further. At a minimum you may learn a few things, and at a maximum this may be a good time to examine some characteristics or behaviors in yourself or someone you care about that could dangerously affect your ability to live a fully loaded grown-up life.

Addiction is one of the most significant categories in this book and in your life, because it has the power to destroy all other nine areas of functioning in one fell swoop. Addiction is defined as the habitual and/or compulsive surrender to a substance or activity. Really it's just a way to run or hide from something—generally feelings; and there are an awful lot of adults out there escaping into the bottle, a pack of cigarettes, a poker game, a sale at the mall, or a supersized bag of chips and soda.

Grown ups who are well balanced and not addicted to anything in particular know it with total certainty. People who are seriously addicted to something—particularly drugs, alcohol, or food—also know it beyond the shadow of a doubt; these tend to be problems that manifest early in life and wreak such havoc that many young men and women are forced to admit they are addicts at a relatively young age. The reality is that deep down inside, when being honest, a true addict knows he's an addict—no matter what he may say or portray to others.

Addiction is an enormously complicated topic, one that is far too large and complex to be addressed in a single chapter of one book. When you know you have an addiction, you need real, concrete help, way beyond what this or any book can provide, and I urge you to seek professional help immediately from either a doctor, counselor, 12-step program, or treatment facility. However, I would like to talk about all those functioning adults in the middle, people who are honestly wondering if they might have a problem or are in the stage of rationalizing and explaining away their behavior. Don't let what could just be something you enjoy, or even a vice, impact your success and functioning and get in the way of the life you dream of!

Three elements come into play to create an addict: genetics, the environment, and the social factor. If one of these is present in your life, you need to be cautious—the seeds of addiction are there. If two of these components are present, there's a higher chance you could become an addict of some sort. If you have all three, it's basically like three strikes in baseball; you need to watch carefully and not succumb.

Family history is crucial when looking at the roots of addiction. When a parent or primary caregiver who is a biological relative is an addict, the child has a genetic predisposition to that substance. Numerous family, twin, and adoption studies have proved that alcoholism, for example, has a definite genetic component; meaning that children of alcoholics are born with a built-in weakness. Children of alcoholics are four times more likely than other children to become alcoholics themselves, and their genes definitely play a part. However, the lines get blurry when it comes to distinguishing between genetic causes and the powerful environmental factors that come into play.

You learn what you live, and if you grew up with a mom who headed for the cupcakes every time she was stressed, or a father who drank away his work problems every night, that's behavior you internalized as a child. Another part of this environmental factor is not only what you saw, but what your caregiver did for you: if you started crying, you might have gotten taken out for an ice-cream cone. If you had a bad day at school, your mother might have said, "Let's go shopping for a new dress; that will cheer you up." If you were taught to escape the uncomfortable feelings you experienced as a child by getting a treat, this was a powerful early lesson in "This feels bad; let's stop all those bad feelings with a quick fix."

Shopping, ice cream, special treats—none of these things in and of itself is bad, but what's missing from this equation is the validation of the child's experience. When you were bullied at school, or wet your pants, or your little boyfriend or girlfriend broke up with you, you were sad or scared or angry or hurt. If your parents were too busy or tired or simply incapable of listening, empathizing, and validating your experiences, some took the easy way out. They shut you up by sticking an ice-cream cone in your hand. They handed you a new toy. Soon enough, as a child, you learned both by watching your parent and experiencing how they handled your problems that this is what you do to make yourself feel better.

A child who grows up in a home with an addict usually finds himself with unpredictable caregivers whose moods and behavior are always changing. One minute he might have the sweetest, caring mother; the next minute he's dealing with a raging, dish-throwing maniac or a zombie passed out on the couch. Not just moods but activities as well become quite erratic—when the parent is having a good day, all is fine at the Little League game—Mom gets the uniform and equipment together, drives to the game on time, and cheers from the stands. On a bad day, she can't get out of bed, and the child is left to fend for himself.

This type of upbringing leaves many grown ups with the unshakable conviction that life is uncertain and, if they are particularly insightful, fearful that they will repeat those destructive patterns. Their ability to trust not only themselves but other people may have been profoundly damaged. It also affects their ability to accurately assess and predict events in their own lives. If you had a chaotic childhood where you never knew what to expect, you will have a hard time planning and predicting events in your grown-up life, or you may work doubly hard to try to do so.

A typical reaction from those who grew up in homes with alcoholics or drug addicts, smokers, or overeaters is that those kids say to themselves: *I will never be like that. I'm not going to do the things my parents do.* Some of them are strong enough and determined enough to forswear that substance forever. But many succumb to the exact same habit—because of the genetic weakness, learned behaviors, or the need to escape. Lo and behold, they find themselves addicted to the exact same thing as their parents. Others hate that their parent smoked constantly and swear they will never go near a cigarette. And they don't—but they do drink to excess, or eat, or shop, or work out compulsively. They have escaped that one particular problem that made their childhood miserable, but they haven't escaped addiction.

The final piece of the pie is the impulsive/social element of addiction. Impulse control has a genetic element; it is also a learned behavior, and those with poor impulse control are far more likely to become addicts. As far as the social element of addiction, birds of a feather flock together—if most of the members of your family are heavy overeaters, or smoke cigarettes, or drink hard, then it's likely you will too. If all of your friends gamble or shop obsessively or live on their iPhones or BlackBerrys, then you will probably do the same, and you'll also be far less likely to think that you have a problem. After all, everybody's doing it.

## Warning Signs

The question that I want you to ask yourself is, is there a substance or activity you engage in frequently that pulls you away from relationships, success, accomplishments, and a full, satisfying life? Let's assess if you have any harmful addictions in your life or not. Take a good hard look: are you relying on something to take you away, ease the pain, or make you feel better? Are you shopping so much that you're in debt or struggling to make ends meet? Are you drinking to the point where hangovers keep you home from work or you got a DUI? Are you eating so much that your weight is a problem—not only in terms of appearance but your health? Can you literally not make it through the day without going through a drive-thru for some fries or stopping off for that after-work drink (or three)? Have you gone way past the point of enjoying numerous sexual partners to having risky sex with strangers out of a compulsive need? Maybe you forgot to TiVo your favorite television show, and you're extremely upset, obsessing about what you missed and when you might be able to watch it. What if you're out at a family dinner and your phone goes off—are you unable to resist the compulsion to see who's reaching out to you and respond? Are your friends and loved ones complaining that you spend more time with your electronics than you do with them?

As I mentioned in the chapter about dynamic communication, I find that technological addiction is a very real phenomenon these days. We all benefit from our ability to multitask and be two places at once. Our laptops, cell phones, BlackBerrys, and all the other devices allow us to stay in touch whenever and wherever we need or want to. You can be at the playground with your children or standing in line at the bank and still be working! You can also be on a blind date and getting advice and coaching on how to escape tactfully without your date even knowing you're e-mailing or texting a friend. People use these devices to maximize their time and stay connected, but overuse can quickly spin out of control. Everybody's doing it—talking on their cell phones while checking out at the market, texting while eating lunch with a friend, surfing the Internet while hearing your friend's latest drama—so most of us are guilty of feeding the frenzy.

This is because humans love to feel connected and enjoy social stimulation and interaction. Given social networking sites, we can now have literally hundreds or thousands of "friends" and communicate with them all day long, receiving updates and going back and forth, when we often should be doing other things. Absolutely, it's a boon for people who are isolated or building a business. In many cases I encourage people to embrace technology for support. It's when you are glued to your computer or mobile device to the exclusion or detriment of everything else—like your family who is in the house with you (often absorbed in their own devices) or your friend sitting across the table—that there's cause for concern.

This can be a very tough habit to break, because we enjoy access 24/7 from anywhere—stuck in traffic, from a mountaintop, you name the most remote location, and I guarantee there's a way to stay in touch with your boss, friends, or family, which was never before possible.

The other great benefit of the information age is that we are now all able to stay on top of breaking news and the very latest scandal, celebrity gossip, fashion blog . . . Many of us have become addicted to the sensation of being in the know and informed of everything, right away—most of it far-from-essential information. It's brain candy, and too much candy can make you sick. The best solution is to set limits on your use of these devices and stick to it. No texting at the table, no laptop in bed . . . but I'm not suggesting you go cold turkey! How about starting by turning your phone off for one lunch with a friend?

But let's cut to the chase here. If you spend more time on your cell phone or BlackBerry than you do with your partner or children, why is that? Why is what's going on there more important or engaging than your friends or family? If you can only make it through each day of work by thinking about lunch and what to buy next out of the vending machines, then what's really happening at your desk? If you spend more time watching television shows or on the computer or playing video games than interacting with your spouse, why don't you want to spend time with him or her? If you are too busy exercising each morning to see your kids off to school, why can't you take a day off? What are you trying to distract yourself from? Why are you avoiding facing your regular life and the people in it?

Whatever is causing you to pull away from other activities in your life needs to be examined. It may not be addiction by definition, but it's definitely getting in the way of your being a fully loaded grown up, and isn't that what we all hope to be? It really comes down to this: how is this substance/behavior harming your life or getting in the way of your success? Addiction has plenty to do with lifestyle and context. A wealthy person can shop and gamble more than a person with a limited income. Someone with a high metabolism who works out every day can eat a lot more than someone who doesn't. A lightweight cannot drink as much as someone with a high tolerance for alcohol who goes out every night. Nothing is black and white; it's about looking for red flags. I encourage you to begin to spend some time looking for them so you can intervene early if there is trouble looming ahead.

# Rationalization

Those who are struggling with a possible addiction are the best rationalizers in the world. These rationalizations allow the addicts to justify and minimize in their own minds what they are doing and offer excuses to other people, so they feel less guilty about their behavior. The excuses are endless: I'm not an addict, because I go to work every day. I don't have to drink; I just do it to relax or when I'm out with my friends. I only gamble twice a year, on trips to Las Vegas. I know I gained ten pounds in the past month, but I'll diet again and lose it. I know I work out three hours a day, but I have to look good for my job, and it keeps me in shape. I drive through fast-food restaurants every day at four o'clock because I don't have time in the morning to prepare a snack for later.

Well, just because you don't drink every day doesn't mean you're not an alcoholic. Just because you ate sensibly for two days doesn't mean you're not a food addict, and just because you don't look at your e-mails on Sunday doesn't mean you're not addicted to your mobile device. I think you get the point.

Guess what—these things can and do make us feel good. A drink does take the edge off. Shopping is fun. Eating is comforting. Connecting with those online or via e-mail or texting is satisfying. That's why any activity can become a slippery slope to addiction. If your behavior is only harming you, that's bad as it is, but if you have a spouse, business partner, or children, and you are supposed to be a role model, good partner, the grown up, then you have a double responsibility to face it and deal with your addiction. You can't rationalize away the fact that your addictive behavior is affecting them. What means more to you than your own desires: your mate, child, pet, parent, job?

We've talked in other chapters about the tapes that roll in our heads and the voices that we hear. These voices can sound like screaming to addicts or those headed down the path of addiction: *I can't handle this. I need to get away. I'm scared. I'm lonely. I have to feel better. I don't care what happens tomorrow, I have to have this, buy this, eat this, do this right now. Why should I deprive myself? I'm not hurting anyone. I can get a second job if I need to make more money to pay for all of this. I'm hungry, and fast food is cheap.*

As the addiction progresses, and whatever substance you're overusing or abusing in your life becomes more and more of a problem, the voices start saying, *I tried to quit, and it was too hard, so I'm just going to do it anyway.* Or, *I blew my diet today, so I might as well eat what I want this week. I already smoked a cigarette; I might as well finish the pack.* There's a lack of ability to start over and a fear of failure in trying. Addicts tend to throw in the towel; it's all-or-nothing thinking.

This can lead to the same problem, but with a different "drug" when addicts try to address their issues; for example, they'll quit smoking and gain fifty pounds, or stop drinking and take up smoking and caffeine in ridiculous amounts. Or they lose fifty pounds but bankrupt themselves with a shopping habit. So goes the cycle: needing a quick fix to escape whatever it is they're feeling. Many just replace one coping mechanism with another. Others are faced with stacking addictions: they smoke when they drink. They are addicted to both drugs and Internet pornography. You can drink, smoke, eat, watch TV, and text a friend all at the same time! Many addictions become intertwined behaviors, which makes them doubly difficult to overcome. The irony with this cycle is that the addict is trying to escape her past, her emotions, her circumstances and even her own self, and yet the substance or habit is only a mask because you can never truly escape your own feelings, situation, or self. Nevertheless, a grown up faces the feelings, no matter how intense, depressing, or anxiety-provoking they are instead of working so hard to escape them.

When it comes to addiction, desire to quit that habit or substance will never be enough. If you were raised in an environment where you were taught that it's fine to escape your feelings, you have to learn how *not* to escape your feelings in order to break the addiction. And that's too scary for many people. The need to escape is driven typically by four key feelings: shame, fear, anger and sadness.

### SHAME—I've stepped into some quicksand.

Shame is the feeling that drives us to want to hide. Many of my clients have described it as a cold wet blanket. It's the feeling that makes you want to stay in bed and never come out from under the blankets. You don't want to talk to or see anyone. Shame makes you hate yourself above and beyond any other feeling. It's the feeling that leaves you grabbing the proverbial baseball bat and beating yourself over the head with criticism. Shame makes you say "I am worthless, no one loves me, I am stupid, I am so embarrassed, I can't control myself."

When it comes to shame tied to addiction, shame leaves you saying things like, "I blew it. I did it again. I am hopeless. I hate myself. I'll never be able to quit." Spending too much time feeling shame is dangerous because shame keeps us stuck. It can drag us lower and lower than ever before, much like stepping into a pool of quicksand. It also makes us want to hide and never come out, so we find various ways to do this—we escape into drinking, taking drugs, shopping, our bed, the sofa.

The only way to pull yourself out of shame is to move. I mean literally, physically *move*. Sticking with the quicksand analogy, if you stepped into it, you'd have to physically start walking or moving to get out so you don't sink! So get out of bed, walk out of the house, your office, the car. Run, jog, get on a bicycle, go to a friend's house. Keep moving until you move into a feeling that is less sticky—which is any other feeling.

**ANGER—I feel like there's a rocket ship taking off in my chest.**

The anger that underlies addiction is directed at both the addict and others. The anger at oneself is perhaps the most dangerous, because you have twenty-four-hour-a-day access to take out that anger. Anger toward others can be somewhat managed by not being around the person we are angry with all the time. The anger rush moves up from your feet to the top of your chest within seconds or milliseconds, and trying to stop an emotion at that speed can be nearly impossible at times. That rush can move you to lash out and do things you might regret. It can make you say things you don't mean, feel things you wouldn't be feeling if you were calm, and behave in ways that you might not normally behave. Anger can be a direct road to shame or back to shame—if you are remorseful at all—and I've already told you how bad shame can be.

Anger says, "I am entitled, I can do what I want, I don't care," and in the moment you are feeling that rush that comes from your drink, your food, your gambling—you really don't care and you really do feel invincible. But guess what? While you are feeling that rush, your body is so busy being angry that your brain doesn't think as clearly, and so your decision-making skills are impaired. The best way to manage the anger you feel is to calm down and turn the rocket into a tricycle—a method of transportation that you can actually get on top of and control.

Count to ten, run around the block, and question whether or not your anger is justified. Think about how you want to behave. Ask yourself if your anger is productive or damaging. Here's a hint: anger that is directed toward making things better—like the anger that got African Americans a seat in the front of the bus or gave women the right to vote—is good and productive because it generates successful outcomes. Anger that is directed toward harming yourself or others—like the anger that makes you run up your credit card because you are mad at your mate or the anger that makes you lash out at your boss—is toxic and unproductive and leads to the downward spiral of failure.

**FEAR—I am jumping out of my skin.**

Fear says, *I don't think I can function without this substance/activity.* It says, *I'm scared to see the type of person that I will be if I stop doing this behavior.* Fear says, *I tried once before; what if I fail again?*

Fear makes us question ourselves and doubt our capabilities, lose trust in who we are, and think we can never reach the level of happiness or success that we aspire to. Fear pulls us toward our addiction as if to say, *I'm so afraid of what I will not have or who I might be that I should drown the pain instead of taking the risk,* and fear fears the idea of failing even one time. Fear makes your body feel prickly, jittery, anxious, as if you can't even stand living in your own skin. It makes you want to fight or flee so that you don't have to sit in that uncomfortable place for even a moment longer. When you feel fear, unlike with shame, I encourage you to feel this feeling, at least for a moment, long enough to ask yourself, *What am I afraid of? Are any of these fears based in reality? Who taught me to be so scared? Is my fear protecting me in any way? Is there another way that I can protect myself?* The chapter on coping talks more about how best to manage fear.

**SADNESS—My heart is so heavy I can barely move.**

Sadness is the heartbreaking driver of addiction. It's that quiet weak voice inside of you that says, *I can't do any better, I'm scared, I'm pitiful, I'm helpless, I'm hopeless.* Sadness often comes from feeling too many failures or having too much abuse directed your way—abuse from yourself, a mate, your parents, anyone who plays or played a significant role in your life. It's the feeling that makes your heart feel so heavy that you don't want to move or feel like you are literally unable to move. It drags you around like a wet blanket of despair. The best way to manage sadness is to get it some support. Reach out to friends, family, and your support group to lift you up and provide you comfort. Also find some goodness inside yourself; pull yourself up from sadness by telling yourself what you like about yourself and what it is you have to offer. Sadness needs comfort. Not the comfort of a drink, a cookie, or a purchase, but the true comfort of a person or group of people who care.

## Assess It and Address It

Let's discuss the tools you can use to determine whether or not you really have an addiction problem.

- **DYNAMIC INTERACTION.** As we discussed in an earlier chapter, all communication starts with you. Every single person I've known who battled an addiction remembers a certain point when a small voice in his or her head, saying, *I think I might be an* . . . (alcoholic, drug addict, compulsive gambler, fill in the blank) became too loud to ignore. Don't ignore this voice; it's trying to tell you something important. This is generally followed by a time of worry and questioning. Do I or do I not have a problem?

- **SUPPORT SYSTEM.** This is where your support group comes in. Ask five trusted people: do you think I shop too much? Do you think I drink too much? If more than one says yes, it's worth seriously examining this problem. You may not have to ask; friends and family, because they care, will be the first to say, "I think you might have a drinking problem." The problems start because the natural first re-action to this is to be defensive. To stop being defensive means to commit to listening. Your response should be, "I heard what you said, and I will think about it." Then walk away. Don't say any more. Go away and think about it. If the feedback you're getting is overwhelming, then you need to pay attention.

- **PROFESSIONAL HELP.** If you've reached the point where you are doing something that is harming you and you can't stop and you know darn well you're an addict, it's time for professional help. You may not have the tools you need to deal with this problem, but somebody else might.

    This involves reaching out—to a medical doctor, a psychiatrist, a priest or rabbi, a 12-step group—because those people will know where to send you. Addicts tend to isolate themselves when they think they're in trouble. This is exactly the time when you must force yourself to reach out and find someone who knows better than you. Shame is what holds too many people back from asking for professional help.

Remember, you don't have to tell anybody in your "real" life about your problem. Go find somebody who's a stranger to tell! Find a different doctor, or an addiction counselor. That's the great thing about 12-step programs—they're anonymous, you don't even have to speak, and they've heard it all before and worse. There is no shame in those rooms, only love and acceptance and understanding.

- **ROLE MODELS.** Throughout this book I speak a great deal about the importance of having just one good role model in your life. When it comes to addiction, it's time to reconsider who is around you. If your addiction is keeping you from living the lifestyle you desire, you need to change the company you keep. You need to make some different friends. You need to go out with people who have one drink, not seven. You need to start hanging out with friends who eat salad, not all-you-can-eat buffets. You need friends who do other things besides shop twenty-four hours a day. If no one you spend time with smokes, it is far less likely that you will smoke. If the people around you are condoning or actively encouraging your bad habits, then you need to get rid of them or minimize the relationship and find new friends and role models. This means rallying a new group, but to start, you only need one role model friend to help.

## The Addict in Your Life

No discussion of addiction would be complete without talking about how other addicts affect your life, even if you're not one yourself. You see the signs, and it's clearly impacting your life and relationship. The bottom line is that addicts will hurt your ability to have a fully loaded life, because that person will only bring you down. If you always have to leave parties early because your partner has passed out or a friend is making an embarrassing scene, or your sister keeps borrowing money to feed her gambling habit or racking up the bills because of her drinking or spending, it's time to look out for your own best interest. Offer help and support, but if it is turned down, protect yourself and change your level of interaction.

If the addict in your life is eating to the point of physical illness that impairs his or her functioning, for example, then I believe you need to intervene. It starts with a conversation, a nonjudgmental, heart-to-heart discussion where you *listen*. If that doesn't work, it might take rallying more friends and family to talk to them. In the end, it's about assessing your own life and whether or not this person should be in it. If the person is continuing to impact your life negatively, he or she may need to be removed from it.

So many brilliant, wonderful, caring people's lives have been destroyed by addiction. If you are struggling with the thought that you may, indeed, have a real problem, I want to congratulate you for facing your demons head-on—like a real grown up. There is no such thing as a hopeless addict. As long as you are living and breathing, you can fix whatever holds you back.

# 10

# I Don't Have
# Time to Read
# This Chapter!

**T**ime heals all wounds. Time is money. One day at a time. Where did the time go? I need more time. Time is on my side. Time flies. Time is of the essence. What time should we meet? What time is it? We're always referring to time, and clocks and watches regulate much of how we live our lives. We have specific times when we eat, times when we meet, times we must arrive at work or make an important call. The stock market opens and closes at a fixed time, there are time zones, time keepers, time slots, and even movie times. You can go into overtime, you can be on time, and your time can be up. What invitation would be sent without a time listed on it? With time playing such a significant role in our lives, you can surely appreciate that it is actually one of our most valuable resources. In terms of being a responsible and reliable grown up, it will help you immensely to recognize this fact and maximize the value of both time and balance.

One of my goals in writing this book is to encourage you to zero in on the factors that may be adversely affecting you and holding you back from a fully loaded grown-up life. So far we've covered many of the areas that impact the happiness and success of your life—jobs, money, addictions, intimate relationships—and hopefully helped you to identify and face up to the existence of any problems. We've also discussed some ways to start down the right path. Now, what you may be thinking when it comes to implementing some of these ideas, because I hear it from men and women all the time, is *I don't have the time to really focus on that* (whatever that may be) *and deal with it*. For example: "I don't have time to work out at the gym and plan healthy meals." "I can't spare the time to see my friends as often as I'd like." "Neither my husband nor I have enough time to go on a date night." "I wish I could spend more time with my kids." Or even, "I don't have time to read this chapter." Do any of these sound familiar?

Far too many people are just rushing through their busy, overloaded lives, never accomplishing what they set out to do that day, let alone adding a new activity to an already overwhelming, exhausting schedule and endless to-do list. My response to that is, Why is it, if we all have the same twenty-four hours in a day available to us, that some people are extremely productive and accomplish any number of amazing things without getting shook, while others can barely make it through their bare minimum of tasks that must be completed each day?

We have come into an age in our society where everybody is in a constant hurry and there are tons of speedy alternatives to help us be ever more time efficient. You can get money fast anywhere from an ATM, quick coffee from drive-through Starbucks, your dry cleaners is open seven days a week, you can pay your bills online where your credit-card information is stored, your cell phone has speed dial so you only have to hit one button, there are preset text messages you can send . . . everything in our lives is set up to save time and speed up, yet people complain more now than ever that they are overloaded, overwhelmed, and exhausted. Again, why is that?

I believe one big factor is that women and men today are trying to pack in so much more than they used to. Gender roles until just the last couple of generations were clearly separated; both men and women had separate duties and, as a general rule, didn't worry about the other's role, because they weren't supposed to or didn't have to. People ages twenty to fifty-five were the first generation to be told that they could do it all and have it all. Women can be CEOs, and men can raise children. We all internalized the ideals, but no one told us how to successfully manage to squeeze it all in. Most of us are doing double the amount of work our grandparents did in a day, because we believe it is not only possible but desirable to do so. Now women have fully absorbed the idea that they can balance careers with family life and have told men that when they come home from their jobs, it's time to change the diapers on the baby and wash some dishes. Everybody has too much on their plates. So much, that most of us need to upgrade to a platter!

However, some enviable people do seem to "do it all"—and the rest of us wonder how. They do it all because they have mastered the art of time management and balance, a critical component in every area of your life. Time management has nothing to do with time. Time management is the group of skills, talents, techniques, and resources that you utilize to accomplish tasks, projects, or goals. The ability to maximize and balance the twenty-four hours we all have in a day will help guarantee your success. The entire message of this book is about taking responsibility for your own life. Time management and balance are two areas that many of us never take responsibility for. We don't even realize that we have given this responsibility away!

Here's how: when you make the statement "I don't have the time," it takes the power away from you and puts it on the clock. It sticks the responsibility for your life onto an outside source, as if time is a force that somehow controls you instead of the other way around. How often have you heard, or said, "There aren't enough hours in the day"? This statement tells the world that the clock determines what you do with your day and, ultimately, your life. The simple truth is, you have time for exactly what you make time for. Your priorities and what you value most make it into the minutes and hours of the day, even if you aren't consciously aware of it, and the lower-priority and lower-valued items get neglected or forgotten altogether.

For example, if you have decided that it's important for you to hold down a job, which requires you to shower, dress appropriately, and look presentable each day when you arrive, you will find the time to prepare and manage to show up each day on time. If you have made the commitment to find a new job or a new mate or a new friend, you will somehow make the time to do that. If you are dying to see that new movie, read that new book, or visit that sale, you'll squeeze it in, no matter how busy you are. Grown ups don't find the time for anything—we all have the same amount of that. They plan, prioritize, and make the time for what matters and for what's important, and they do it consciously. The only way to do that is to take ownership of your own schedule, and I will help you do that.

Are you one of those people constantly bemoaning how they have no time? If so, why are you always saying that? Is it a bad habit? Do you want others to sympathize with all your burdens and let you off the hook? Are you hoping to be cut some slack? Did you not even realize that you were doing it before I mentioned it here? Are you really overloaded and unable to cope and this is the only way you can express it—it's easier to say, "I don't have time"? Are you constantly making excuses? Excuses are most frequently made when a person doesn't want to take responsibility, needs an out or pity, or out of habit. This could be anything from "I don't have a reliable car" to "I don't wear a watch" to "I'm totally disorganized" or even "There was a long line at the ATM, and I was out of cash." These particular excuses are about practical things, but they still may be getting in the way of time management. Let's say you waste a lot of time every morning searching for your car keys because you tend to lose things a lot—it's time to turn to another book to get some skills and focus on this particular problem. Losing items is costing you time and aggravation each morning but, more important, it may eventually cost you a job or significant relationship.

If you didn't take it in when I mentioned it earlier, you need to absorb it now because it is the most critical bit of content in this book. Every time you say you have no time or make excuses, whatever your reason is for saying it, you lose ownership of your own life and hand over your power and control to your clock. Instead, say phrases like, "I am working on reorganizing my schedule," or, "Some priorities have fallen off my radar, and I need to get them back on," or, "There is so much that is important to me; I am trying to reorder what comes first these days." These sentences, and others like them, are action oriented and will redirect your focus to what needs to be fixed instead of putting energy toward what you cannot change—the fact that there are only twenty-four hours in a day!

There are many time-management books, workshops, systems, and lectures everywhere—some are really excellent (see my suggestions at the end of this book). If you do not have the skills, tools, and resources, don't just throw your hands in the air and say you don't know how or can't manage. Go find out how to develop the skills— it can be done. That's what fully functioning, successful adults do. Entire stores in your local mall are filled with gadgets that will save you time in every area of your life. These are all great tools but only if you use them in combination with all that we have discussed. They will not work if you transfer what you are responsible for onto a device—your PDA, your electronic calendar, your alarm clock.

This chapter is not the place to get into the how-tos. It's about asking you to take a look at the most valuable things you have: your twenty-four hours, 365 days a year of time, and how you choose to own it, control it, take power over it, and manage it. You are responsible for every waking moment. And that means juggling the demands you get from the people you work with, those who are close to you (family, mate, and friends) and the demands you make on yourself. I want you to stop defining time as something that is taken away from you, that costs you, that you can never get enough of, instead of looking at the choices you make about how to fill your time.

This is really about saying, I choose to work at this job that sometimes demands long hours and working lots of overtime, because I value stability and a good income. I choose to have friends who want to see me, and I make the time to show up for them when they ask or need me to, because a good group of friends and support system are important. I choose to take the time to relax and recharge however I want—whether that's reading a book, taking a hike, or going to the gym each night—because it helps me unwind. I choose to have date nights with my partner because I enjoy them and they help us connect.

Okay, I trust you've gotten the point by now! Back to your schedule. As a general rule of thumb, most adults need seven hours of sleep a night, and work eight to nine hours a day, five days a week. Let's be generous here and give you sixteen hours for both work and sleep. That leaves you eight hours each day—generally more on weekends; how do you want to divide that up? As we discussed in the chapter on coping, these hours and your desired activities are your cards to play. How do you want to play them? Is it your priority to spend four hours working out? Do you want to spend five hours lying on the couch watching television every night after work? Do you need to learn new skills and wish you could take a class? Want to cook more? Go out more? Invest more time in building a support system or cultivating an intimate relationship? Grown ups think about what is important to them and their schedule in advance, and they plan and prioritize so they are able to fit in what matters most.

Let's make a chart. First, list the five activities or people in your life that are your top priorities. Those might include work, your child, your spouse or dating, caring for family or friends, exercise and/or socializing, taking a class, enjoying your favorite hobby or sport. Run through the past two weeks in your mind and figure out what you've spent the bulk of your time doing—have you been doing these five things you listed as priorities? If not, what five things have you been spending the most time doing?

It's important to take a look at your complete daily schedule— one schedule for weekdays and one for the weekend. Where is your time going? Is your time productive or wasted? Are you investing time and energy in the areas that are really most in line with your values and desires? Is anyone or anything that you consider important being neglected or ignored by how you allot your time?

Here's how this process should work: once you carefully examine your daily life, schedule, and needs, it will soon become apparent that whatever is most valuable to you, you manage to make happen—you will not only fit in what's important, but you will be a role model for others. When you take ownership of your life and the time you have while living it, there will be some priorities that you will make happen; others that fall by the wayside. Those that you don't make happen tell me—and should now begin to tell you—that they're really *not* priorities. Either someone has convinced you they should be priorities for you, you aren't making them priority enough, or you have a fantasy that you will somehow get them all done. But don't kid yourself, because you're not getting them all done.

When you are not making time for the activities you claim are important or wish you had time for, identify which is the first to get lost. Is it your spouse? your children? the occasional lunch with friends? Let's make a list of the first, second, and third things to go when you get overwhelmed. It might look something like this: gym, going out with friends, spending time with spouse. Even the most organized, together people have times when they are overburdened and busier than usual. Are you okay with these things dropping off, or do you feel guilty about it? What stays and what goes in times of stress and overload?

Examining both the taking on of certain roles and setting precedents and limits can be extremely helpful when learning time management and balance. What roles do you want to take on in your living arrangement, for example? Who do you want to be, and what are you willing to do? I always tell people when they enter into any living situation, whether it's a romantic relationship or just a platonic roommate arrangement, be careful what tasks you take on at the beginning, because they might be yours until the end. If you do all the housework and cleaning and cooking, those duties can forever after be considered "yours." If you take out the trash and mow the lawn, very soon those will probably be considered "your" exclusive responsibilities. I hear husbands and wives complain all the time that they never wanted to be the ones to plan the vacations, pay the bills, cook the meals, but it somehow became their role. Call it a pattern, call it a habit—getting those set roles changed can be a challenge. If you've taken on too many, you need to consider how to improve the situation and renegotiate what you've been doing.

Role patterns and habits also develop in your workplace or community. When connecting with any group, think carefully about what roles and duties you are willing to take on, and have a plan in place before you arrive about how you will fill your time, because other people soon expect you to behave predictably. They have expectations too. People in your life can see what you are willing and capable of doing and begin to expect it. If these efforts are directed toward them, very soon it becomes the standard that they will fully expect you to live up to all the time—for the duration of the relationship, not just at the beginning.

Whatever it is that you've decided to shoulder—whether it's commitments at your child's school or plans with a friend—think on it long and hard before agreeing too quickly to do it. If everyone knows you spend all your free time making projects for your kid's school or baking for bake sales or planning all the holiday parties at work for the entire office, these tasks can become your responsibility forever, when you never intended to take them on to start with! Next thing you know, you'll have more items in your schedule to manage!

## No More Excuses!

Here are a few typical responses to the stress of poor time management:

- **BAIL OUT.** This is when tension becomes so overwhelming that right in the middle of a project or travel to a meeting or obligation, you simply give up. You quit the project, turn around, and drive home or miss the meeting or event. You might abandon tasks or even leave jobs because you just can't get a grip on managing your time properly.

- **NO-SHOW.** Different from bailing out on a commitment, this behavior is more along the lines of "I'm not even going to try." When you're asked to a function or event you know you're already too overwhelmed with demands to attend, no matter how beneficial or fun it might be, you don't even try to figure out a way to make it work in your schedule. Similarly, if you are asked to help with an activity, assignment, or project, you turn the request down before there's even a moment of consideration.

- **OVERCOMPENSATION.** You feel you have to apologize numerous times and fall all over yourself to make up for your lateness or poor time management. Not only have you been late or delivered something after a deadline passed, you end up wasting more time and energy overcompensating for this behavior—buying lunch, complimenting the other person, whatever it takes to ingratiate yourself and make up for your poor time management.

- **TAKE A BEATING.** You relentlessly beat yourself over the head and berate yourself about your disorganization and lack of time-management skills. The mistake has already been made, and you've already suffered the consequences, yet you continue to beat yourself up over the incident. The tapes start to roll, and the negative thoughts kick in: *You always do this. You're going to lose your job. They're never going to forgive you for missing that party.*

- **BLAME.** This is constantly shifting the responsibility for your time-management problems onto other people. *I was late because I had to get my kid ready for school. My husband was running behind. My boss didn't give me enough time to get this done. The traffic was horrible.* Beating yourself up is taking on too much responsibility; constantly

shifting blame to another person or circumstance is dis-
owning your responsibility.

Can you relate to this problem of your time being filled with
tasks you took on begrudgingly or never actually wanted to do? Are
there things that you have ended up doing because you felt you
couldn't say no? Did you actually even utter the word "yes," or do
you feel that this task was thrust upon you by a pushy or needy person? If you have answered yes to any of these questions, then you
might be what I call a never-say-no person. Never-say-no people
end up with a full schedule that is based on the priorities of other
people, schools, offices, and organizations instead of their own.
These individuals struggle to juggle the needs and wants of others
while neglecting their own.

This behavior comes out of either baggage or habit is rooted in
fear. We have talked enough about baggage that you realize your
being a never-say-no person has come out of experiences from your
past—probably going all the way back to childhood. If you engage
in this behavior out of habit, maybe it's just the way you've always
behaved and didn't even realize it until you reached a breaking
point. If you behave this way out of fear, is it fear of failure? Fear of
not being liked or accepted? Fear of losing something or someone
you value? Fear of not getting something (a job, a mate, a friend, a
raise, the better teacher)?

If you are one of these people who is now looking at what's on your
plate and seeing that you need to hand off some items, know that it's
not too late. Let people or groups know that although you like them
and want to help, you need to reprioritize your life because your
personal responsibilities are being neglected. Help them create a
plan for you to pass off what you can no longer do so that they are not
left burdened by your newfound realization.

## Learn to Delegate!

Delegation is a key element in mastering time management and balance in your life. This is also where your support system comes in. When you are looking at your priorities and your schedule, the time may be way overdue for you to delegate or hand off some of the items that you cannot physically or emotionally take care of all the time. You may need to find a babysitter to allow for time for yourself or a date with your mate. You may need to hire a professional to create a meal plan, because you don't know how to design one that's healthy. You may want to recruit a teenager to file your bills, convince a friend who is a terrific shopper to help you find clothes that look good on you more quickly, pay the kid next door to wash your car, or even take turns with a friend going grocery shopping each week so you both only have to go every other week!

In the final chapter, we will talk in more detail about how flexibility and creativity help in time management. For the time being, start with the simple question: do you delegate enough? At all? If not, what are you willing to hand off in your life so that you have time to take care of people and activities that are higher priorities? If your answer here is that you can't delegate anything, it must all be done by you, then I encourage you to approach one or two close friends or coworkers and ask them to look at your life and help you delegate. As I told you in the support-system chapter, sometimes we need others to be our mirror to help us see what we can't.

All grown ups have the same balancing act: to juggle the main elements of their lives. For most of us, at a minimum we need to juggle and balance work and/or childrearing, family/intimate relationships/friends, and taking care of ourselves. Balance must begin with taking the time to eat well, stay healthy, and sleep enough, at least most of the time—if your "machine" isn't running well, how can it function efficiently to run your life? Balance is about sometimes going out with friends or loved ones, forgetting your cares, and having a great night out, but also buckling down and being serious when your life and its priorities require you to be. It's about looking at your schedule and ensuring that you have a variety of activities that are important to you and the time to do them all most or all of the time. It's about planning and prioritizing and not committing to more than you can handle versus flying by the seat of your pants in crisis mode, putting out the fires as they begin to burn.

Now, maybe you're thinking, *I can't* or *There are too many people or commitments pulling at me*, or, *Oh, I couldn't let someone else do that—I have to take care of it myself.* In my book (and what I teach and how I live my life as well) there is no such thing as *can't*. "Can't" is a word that takes your power away. You *can* balance everything and find time for everything that matters—if you choose to do so, if you plan and strategize, and if you delegate to your support system and get their help. Like everything else, you have to work hard at it, but it's worth it. Otherwise, you will eventually burn out.

## Maximum Capacity

Maximum capacity isn't something that is just for roller coasters, elevators, and scales. We each have a maximum capacity too. There comes time for each of us when we have reached our limit, we're done, we've had it—we simply cannot take on one more responsibility or commitment. Maximum capacity is different for each individual. Each of us has our own personal breaking point based on who we are and our coping, balance, and time-management skills. Do you know when you've reached yours? How do you act when your breaking point is fast approaching? Do you eat or drink too much? Do you withdraw and become sullen and noncommunicative? Do you act like a put-upon martyr? Furthermore, what do you do when you've reached maximum capacity? Do you mope around? Do you suffer in silence for as long as you can stand it, then explode into a rage or burst into tears? Or do you rally your support system and start handing off work to others?

Although we all have moments when we retreat into our misery or lose it, to the point of feeling like our head is spinning, the goal is to react to reaching our limit in a productive and evolved way. Grown ups who are high functioning rally their support system, take a vacation, set boundaries with those around them, and, most important, they take responsibility for their reaching maximum capacity. After all, if your schedule or life is overbooked and you are overloaded, how did it get that way? It got that way because you allowed it to. You own your own time and how you spend it, and you either took on too much or gave too little away. Additionally, other people will push you just as far as you let them, whether that's in your romantic life, at your office, or in a crowd of strangers waiting in line. It is up to every grown up to know when to draw the line. Refusing to set boundaries tells others that it's okay to expect what they are demanding of you, because your silence is tacit acceptance. What we permit is what we teach.

## It's Very Dangerous to Mismanage Time

The consequences of burnout are very real. It's more than just "stressful" being overloaded; it's actually dangerous to your health, emotional well-being, and relationships! Have you ever been running late and heard yourself say, "I know Tom is going to kill me for being late," or, "My entire career depends on this presentation getting in on time," or, "I'm so late that maybe I should just call and cancel or say I'm sick"? These thoughts are driven by fear of the worst-case-scenario outcome.

The biggest problem with these emotions is the physiological component of fear. When the human body is afraid, it kicks into fight-or-flight mode. The blood rushes to your extremities—away from your brain and into your arms and legs. Your heart and pulse rate go up, and your mind begins to race. These changes are great if you are actually running to finish a marathon, but the marathon of life is harmed by these changes. When all of this is going on in your body, your mind can't think as clearly, you lose focus, and then you lose the ability to stay centered. This can cost you *more* time, just when you need it most.

Study after study has proved that people who are rushing are more likely to injure themselves and get into car and household accidents. When you're not on time and feeling out of balance, you are distracted, upset, anxious, rushed, and more likely to take risks. This, along with the adrenaline reaction, will decrease your ability to react quickly and think clearly, hugely raising your chances of getting into trouble, whether that means losing your keys, accidentally hurting yourself, foolishly speeding, or getting into a car accident. These situations are exactly when all your papers fall out of your arms, you accidentally crash into a pole, you forget to bring part of your presentation—and then guess what? The fear escalates even more, and the downward spiral begins as the body floods with still more adrenaline.

It is critical to manage the fear even more than the time, first by recognizing and acknowledging that your time-management issues are driven by some kind of fear—of being judged, of not being good enough, that you really will be unable to get it all done. Second, you must learn to talk to the fear and calm it down. You need to relax your physical body with deep breathing and relaxation techniques, and then you need to focus your mind, so you can slow it down and think more clearly and function more efficiently, thus making you more likely to correctly manage the time that you have.

My friend is a wardrobe stylist who works on some of the most prestigious fashion shows in the world with many famous celebrities and supermodels. This would certainly qualify as one of the most high-pressure jobs imaginable. I've asked him many times, "How do you do it? How do you manage all those egos backstage, the girls and their clothing changes in such a rush? How do you not rip off a button or snag nylons?" He always replies, "We don't rush. The best way to do something quickly is to do it methodically and correctly the first time." Those models who have one minute to change? They move fast, but they move efficiently and carefully. Haste makes waste. In the world of high fashion, and in your world too.

## Always Running Behind

I've just touched on a problem that is endemic in our society: lateness. Personally, it drives me crazy when somebody shows up late for a meeting with me, holding a fresh, steaming-hot coffee drink from a coffee shop. This tells me that she put getting her caffeine jolt ahead of being on time to see me. Now you may argue that this coffee-carrying person needed a quick pick-me-up before our appointment. Well, guess what? I needed one too, so I got up ten minutes earlier to get my caffeine fix so I would arrive on time.

Whether it's coffee buying that made you late or you just overslept, regular tardiness sends a very bad signal to others. It says that this event or meeting is not your priority—that sleep or coffee came first. Chronic tardiness tells people that they don't matter, and this bad habit can impact your social and business relationships to the point of costing you a friendship or even a job.

Obviously, I am not talking about rare or emergency situations here, where you were held up in traffic by an accident, or your child had a problem at school you needed to deal with immediately, or your boss called a last-minute meeting that made you late. I am talking about habitually running behind and constantly scrambling to get to the next place. How many times have you sat through a meeting or even lunch with a friend where your companion is distracted and can't relax because she's already running late for her next appointment? There she is frantically texting and calling and arranging other plans on what is supposed to be "your" time.

Busyness and lateness have become acceptable in our world, where we're all so crazy busy, overextended and important. "I didn't call you back because I was busy." "I couldn't make it; I was too busy." "I'm late because I am overloaded." "You know me, I took on too much, and it ended up impacting you again; I'm so sorry!" If something is a priority for you, you make it happen. If I convince you of anything in this chapter, it needs to be that. You own your time. Make important people and activities a high priority. Prove to them and you that they are, by fitting them in on a regular basis.

The first step, obviously, is being aware of what you want and deciding to get it done; the second step is about delivering on that commitment. Do you follow through? Successful adults not only lay out workable plans; they deliver. When your time-management and balance skills are poor and you are frequently unable to deliver on what you say you'll do, the fallout will impact every area of your life: your support system, your intimate relationships, and your career, to name a few. Most people prefer to be around and spend their time with a grown up who is reliable and responsible, someone who can be counted on—don't you?

## Wasting Time

Even if they consider themselves to be on top of their schedules and obligations, very few people realize just how much time they waste! Everybody has a favorite time waster, and most of us need one every once in a while: Do you hang out in bars and drink? Do you zone out in front of the TV? Do you play on the Internet? Do you watch every video on YouTube? Hopefully, listing your schedule helped you to identify the main time wasters in your own life.

Time wasters can serve as a necessary and harmless stress reliever and form of escape from time to time. But you need to examine whether these time wasters are affecting your life, taking away from those activities or individuals you consider important. If they are, you need to spend less time on the time wasters and more time on what you labeled a priority.

Likewise, taking a hard look at your schedule and time wasters can be an excellent early indicator of a warning sign of addiction: how much time are you spending on an activity or substance . . . too much? Take a look back at the chapter on addiction. Again, if this is the root cause of your time-management/balance problems, it's time to focus on and address this particular area.

What if the world at large tells you that you're doing something they think is a waste of time but you find necessary, fun, and/or rewarding? Like watching sports on television, for example, or having long heart-to-heart chats with friends on the phone. What others, including your significant others, view as time wasters may or may not be in your mind, and here's where your trusted person or mirror comes in. Do people complain that you do too much of something? If you can't answer this question on your own, this is where a reality check from "your person" comes in. If you're hearing it from that one, and, even worse, if it's impacting him or her and hurting your relationship, then you need to reassess your priorities.

## The End Game

When many of us think about time management, we think about the twenty-four-hour cycle. I hope you have discovered in this chapter that time management is really about your life and not the hours in a day. A successful grown up looks back on each day, month, year, and decade and has an overall sense of satisfaction about how he or she has filled that time.

My goal for you is to feel good about what you've accomplished and how you've spent your precious moments. If you want to spend time with your friends or family, will you look back and regret that you spent most of it at work? If you want to travel the world and see new places, will you realize that you spent most of your time at home? Make it a priority to be able to look back and reflect on your past and feel a sense of joy instead of regret. Work toward managing your time so that when you ask yourself if you spent your time wisely, your answer will be an enthusiastic YES!

## TYPES OF TIME MANAGERS

There are several general types of time managers/time balancers:

**"NEVER SAY NO" PEOPLE.** All they do is say yes, yes, yes. This quality can be quite endearing to others, but it often leaves these time managers neglecting things that they value and also feeling overextended and stressed.

**"DON'T COUNT ON ME" PEOPLE.** All they do is say no. People and organizations learn to not even ask them. This quality allows people to get a lot of their own things done, but it often leaves them without help or support when they need it.

**"I'LL DO IT; WHAT'S ONE MORE THING" PEOPLE.** They live by the credo, If you want something done, give it to a busy person. They are typically highly productive and overloaded, taking little time to relax and have fun.

**"LET ME CHECK MY SCHEDULE" PEOPLE.** They know the importance of balance and time management and don't want to commit without being sure they can reprioritize their schedule. These individuals are typically able to actually be efficient and take time to relax because they are thoughtful about how they plan their time and what they are trying to accomplish.

# 11

# Flex Appeal:
# Bend Before
# You Break

**magine a world with no flexibility.** Every supermarket sells only one brand of soap, cereal, and bread. The streets all run one way. You are assigned a rote job with fixed hours. If you show up for work early or late, you're not allowed in; every business runs exactly on time. Everyone lives in identical houses—all of which are painted regulation slate blue and decorated with the same furniture. Everyone drives the same kind of car. You must only wave hello with your left hand in a back and forth motion. There is only one language permitted, both spoken and written. One acceptable way to dress and walk. There is one kind of money. One acceptable mate. One kind of car and one type of school.

Is it as hard for you as it is for me to imagine living in a world like this? If your answer is yes, that's because life would be ridiculously dull and monotonous in the above scenario. We are fortunate to live in a time where there is freedom of choice, creativity is celebrated, and we all enjoy nearly limitless options. If you consider your own day-to-day life, think for a moment about how frequently you exercise your freedom of choice and take advantage of the flexibility life has to offer.

What's for breakfast? Whatever I feel like having, as long as it's accessible! Should I drive, walk, carpool, or take public transportation to work? It's up to me! Should I watch television, grab a bite with friends, or work out this evening? I can do all three if I want to! Do I want to buy blue ink pens or black? I'm buying red! Work as a firefighter or business executive? I'll be a firefighter until I'm thirty and then switch careers! You see, now that you are an adult, you get to make these decisions and many others 24/7, 365 days a year!

Remember as a child longing for the opportunity to have freedom of choice? What little boy or girl didn't wish to have just one more cookie or that amazing new game, but the caretaker said no? And what teenager didn't wish for an extended curfew, wear what parents considered "an inappropriate outfit," or have ten more dollars to go out? How about just one opportunity in your young life to sit your parents down, tell them everything that you wanted and didn't want, and have them be open to hearing you out and considering bending on at least some of the rules and restrictions?

I certainly remember, when I was growing up and living under my parents' roof, how I pushed them on a regular basis to give me more freedom and flexibility than they were willing to allow and pestered them to let me take on more responsibility than they felt I was ready for. Sorry, Mom and Dad—consider this my official written apology! I know I could be relentless. But, Mom and Dad, what you and so many other parents out there don't seem to understand is that I wasn't looking for you to give me permission to do everything under the sun—though that would have been nice. I was just looking for some more freedom for myself and flexibility from you! Pushing the limits is part of our "job" as adolescents—any parenting book or developmental model on childhood will tell you so. Teens struggle to express their individuality and assert their independence and will push tirelessly for flexibility and understanding from those around them to achieve that mission.

Think back to your own high school days. If you were anything like me and millions of other teenagers out there, you spent your adolescence begging for more leeway in your life. I hope you can also reflect back now from your current vantage point and be honest with yourself: in all likelihood, you weren't as mentally and emotionally prepared to handle that longed-for freedom as you thought you were. You should be now. Ideally, as grown ups, we all should have the emotional and intellectual capacity to work within the flexibility and freedom that adulthood allows us. The problem, of course, is that some of us grant ourselves a little too much leeway or constrict ourselves in a very inflexible manner; hence we are not getting maximum benefit from what life has to offer. This chapter is intended to help you do just that!

**In the chapter on coping we used the analogy of life being like a** card game and the idea that as an adult, you have the unique opportunity of trading in your cards. If there were no flexibility in this world, we'd all be stuck forever with the deal we got at birth. For some of us, that hand we were dealt as children was bad enough that if we were stuck holding it forever, we'd surely leave the table and game! Fortunately, we're not stuck, and we are free every day to choose to improve our hand . . . which is why flexibility is such a key element to being a grown up.

Most of us can intellectually recognize flexibility as a desirable trait. If asked, a majority of people would probably say, and we'd all like to believe, that we are flexible. If challenged, we would point out that we eat different kinds of foods, travel different ways around town, vacation somewhere different each year, or meet different kinds of people all the time. But flexibility goes far beyond that— it is the ability to adapt, change, and conform to any situation—the good and the bad, the planned and the unexpected. It provides us with a skill set that allows us to accommodate any condition, circumstance, or person in the most productive and relaxed manner possible. In other words, to go with the flow—as easily and pain-lessly as possible while maximizing the benefits!

Though we pay lip service to the idea, the reality is that few of us ever give flexibility much thought when it comes to ourselves. Given more pressing issues or personal areas of improvement we would like to address, it's rare to take the time to really examine how flexible you might or might not be. We all certainly take note of other peoples' tendency to be rigid—we quickly realize that they only wear one brand of shoes, drive one kind of car, or socialize with or hire a certain type of person. Maybe you've heard friends say, "I will only travel to places where there is a beach," or, "I never go away without my pillow," or maybe it bugs you when your friend reminds you, "I only accept calls before seven p.m."

Since the entire premise of this book is to examine yourself first, let's take a look at flexibility this way: how flexible you are yourself, and then how your flexibility tendencies may be helping or hurting you. Again, the more you know about yourself, how you operate in your world, and what your strengths and weaknesses are, the better you can harness your knowledge and better your life!

## Evolving and Flexibility

First, let's go all the way back to Darwin's scientifically accepted theory of evolution and natural selection for a moment, which could be loosely translated into: the strong adapt and survive. That's what this chapter is about. Sometimes life throws you really diffi-cult, challenging, or horrible obstacles. If you are unable to cope, as we discussed in the coping chapter, and learn to adapt and be flexible as we will discuss here, then in evolutionary terms you won't survive. In real life, you will not thrive.

That's why it's so important to tune up your flexibility skills now—so you can handle what life throws at you. Just the fact that you are reading this book, examining yourself, and exploring the possibility of becoming more of a grown up tells me that you already have some ability to be open-minded and flexible. If anything you have read so far has made you think and spurred you to take action and address some issues, then that shows me that you have a high level of flexibility. In other words, openness to improving yourself, taking advantage of opportunities, and the willingness and motivation to build on your strengths are all ways that fully loaded grown ups stretch themselves to better their lives.

What if you have decided that flexibility isn't something you care to cultivate—you like the structured, inflexible life you live? You don't want to invest the time and energy into growing your bendability? Then you are familiar with the opposite of flexibility—rigidity. Being rigid will impede you from expressing creativity and exploration, both very valuable pursuits. Being rigid may also prevent you from breaking bad habits, learning new skills, growing relationships, and reaching your full potential.

Some people, of course, are such free spirits that nothing and no one can anchor them to the real world enough so that they want to hold a job, pay taxes, or rent an apartment. Grown-up behavior will never be desirable to them. This sort of person floats through life with as few commitments and responsibilities as possible. As a group, they may be extremely charming people, but they have probably taken flexibility and going with the flow a bit too far for most of us.

In short, either extreme can stop you from evolving, and isn't that what this book and life are all about? However, if none of this sounds appealing to you, or you are worrying that it will take too much effort, know that your decision will ultimately impact you and no one else.

✳ ✳ ✳

**So let's look at your flexibility. If you're not sure how flexible you** are, here are a couple of easy questions to get you started thinking. Would you be disappointed if you didn't get good feedback on an assignment? What if you took all day to cook a meal and it ended up tasting bad? Do you have your own particular way of doing things that you refuse to deviate from? If you veer off course from your plans, does this add great stress to your day, or can you shrug it off? Have people close to you ever called you controlling or a perfectionist?

Let me confess right here: I have perfectionist and controlling tendencies myself, especially in terms of organizing my schedule and my aspirations to meet my goals in a particular way. Any of you who share these qualities should at least acknowledge and be aware of these traits and recognize that they bring both costs and benefits to your life. On the plus side, those of you with similar traits will likely have high expectations and will apply constant pressure on yourself to perform well. You will likely drive yourself hard and set specific goals that you will work to meet in a focused and directed way.

On the minus side of this equation, you are likely a person who prefers to maintain control, has a hard time relaxing and letting go, and tends to feel more stress and anxiety than the average person. You also may struggle with relationships because people tend to shy away from those who appear controlling. Also, there's a tremendous irony in the fact that those of us who tend to be high performing, overachieving perfectionists who place a high premium on success are usually less flexible. Yet those who are less flexible tend to be less successful! This tricky dichotomy requires driven and rigid perfectionists to be vigilant in maintaining some degree of flexibility. It is a form of self-sabotage to master so many positive behaviors that lead toward success yet cripple all that work with the lack of ability to bend. It's like driving with one foot on the brake and the other on the gas!

Another big minus is that rigidity creates so much internal stress, conflict, and anxiety, because you are constantly thinking and managing and planning how to accommodate your needs. Are you often worrying about what you are going to eat at the restaurant before you even get there? Avoiding visiting a friend because she has a child or a dog? Refusing to be friends with someone because he has different interests? Not wanting anyone to touch your desk/wash your dishes/adjust your computer (because they won't do it right)? Do you live in constant fear of being pushed out of your comfort zone?

Hopefully if you have recognized that you happen to be an extremely rigid person, you have many other good qualities going for you, because inflexibility can be a tough trait for others to handle. They must be willing to spend their own time and energy accommodating you, and hopefully they are able to say, "Well, she's so smart (or funny, or accomplished, or capable) that I accept her inflexible nature." Have you ever heard somebody say, "This is just me; this is who I am." A lot of people think that this is an empowering, boundary-setting statement, but it can also be a way of being inflexible and pushing others away. Remember, inflexibility wins the battle, but never the war. When you behave in an inflexible way, you are only focusing on short-term victories or desires you want granted now—but you are probably not examining the after-effects of the damage.

We've all been out to dinner with a person who has very fixed ideas about what it is she will and will not eat and how her food should be prepared. This person quizzes the waiter endlessly about substitutions and ingredients, asks a million questions, takes forever to order, and is never quite satisfied with what is eventually served. Meanwhile, the rest of the table can only hope the waiter doesn't spit in everyone's food along with this person's. Some people call this picky, or particular, or getting what they paid for—but what it is, is inflexible. A flexible adult is one who is able to adapt to a restaurant menu, and does so without making a fuss.

Continuing the food theme, everybody's had that guest at a dinner party who announces, "I don't eat salmon," or, "I'm a vegan," or, "I'm allergic to dairy," at the last minute. It is my belief that real grown ups show up for the dinner party, behave graciously, and eat around whatever particular items they want or need to avoid. If the host is a close friend, you can certainly mention your food preferences in advance, but if he or she is not and you're at the table, you should not make your host or hostess uncomfortable. These two small but common examples are minor in the grand scheme of things—unless, of course, the dinner party was at, say, your boss's house or that of someone whose opinion of you could impact your life. Dinner-party behavior is minor but illustrative of certain behaviors that may need to be addressed or at a minimum examined.

Just as you would not like to live in an inflexible world, potential friends, romantic partners, and employers do not particularly care to be around notably rigid people. Being rigid will make it much more difficult to make friends, hold your job, date, and maintain an intimate relationship. Everybody appreciates some back-and-forth and give-and-take, which tend to be in short supply when you're married to, good friends with, or working with a rigid person or "control freak."

I realize it's tough to develop flexibility if by temperament you tend to be an unbending, less adaptable person, but this skill is an important element for success in everything you do and can be learned. In this chapter, I hope to show you just how beneficial working on this area of your life will be. Let's take a minute to look at the roots of inflexibility.

Sometimes it's just an ingrained habit that has hardened over time. Many people will say, "I need to have my home, car, desk . . . whatever . . . just this way—and if it's not, then I can't function." Maybe your whole life growing up, your mother served dinner at five o'clock on the dot—so you only feel comfortable as an adult eating at five. Maybe you've been taking the same route to work for ten years or had movie night with your spouse on Saturday night since high school, so you gradually have become inflexible when it comes to this particular habit and are upset at any deviation in your particular routine.

Consider your own need to have things stay the same. Think back to when you were in school, or what happens when you take a class, attend meetings, or sign up for a workshop now. On the first day you enter the room, you find a seat and sit down. The next day, do you sit somewhere else, or do you return to the same seat, that day and for the duration of the class? Do you have a regular spot where you sit when you take a break at work? How about a spot where you prefer to sit at home? One particular spot on the couch or a certain side where you feel most comfortable in bed?

Research studies have shown over and over that people seek sameness and routine because it provides comfort. The very things that cause us to feel secure and comfortable are the opposite of flexibility. When it comes to where you sit or sleep or what side of the couch is most indented because you live in that spot, there isn't a tremendous impact on your progress or success in life. I simply mention this phenomenon to keep you thinking about how rigidity and flexibility play a big role in your life on a daily basis. Life itself is unpredictable, and people tend to get set into a certain way of living their lives. A life-changing event like having a child, marrying, taking a new job, moving, or even rearranging your furniture can throw off the program you have set for living your life, and as an adult, you need to be aware that this can happen and plan accordingly.

Emotions and baggage from our pasts drive us toward being rigid. Here are several common places from which this battle to be flexible may have originally sprung:

> **FEAR.** As we have already discussed in other chapters, fear is a polarizing feeling that leads us to either constrict or lash out. Anytime people are driven by fear, they will instinctively move to a rigid position unless they are able to rationally reason with and control their emotions. Do you ever fear the anxiety or stress you feel if something doesn't happen the way you want/need/expect? Do you live in fear of making mistakes or not getting something done? Do you fear getting angry or making someone else angry? Do you fear being judged, failing, or the unknown? If you experience any or most of these in your life on a regular basis, you need to spend some time and energy toward acting on your rational thoughts instead of allowing your feelings of fear to take over. Rational thoughts will allow you to make a plan and follow through despite the discomfort and fear you are feeling.

> **POWER AND PRIDE.** Remember this from the intimate relationships chapter? The harmful aspect of pride shows up as the need to always be right and manifests itself in the fear of being wrong. Are you someone who hates to be

wrong? Do you frequently have a hard time apologizing? Do you find it nearly impossible to see another's point of view? Are you generally intolerant of habits and lifestyles that are different from your own? Have you been referred to as a "control freak"? Do you live by the maxim "It's my way or the highway"? At work or with your spouse or person you're dating, do you say things like, "Hey, I'm not changing for anybody. This is how I am, so deal with it." This is closely related to the need to be right versus the need to get along. You may very well always be right, and you may never change for anybody, but you may be lonely much of the time too.

**REBELLION.** Have you bent over backward most of your life and feel like you are now "owed" something for having made it through those experiences? Were you raised in a household where you were abused and controlled and now you feel a need to rebel against that to finally have things your way? Are you fed up with being treated badly and compromising and now feel compelled to make others do the bending? Have you reached the point where you care more about getting what you want than about your job, your family, or your friends?

Rebellion feels wonderful for some—in the moment. It can feel like a rush, a thrill, intense satisfaction. But with rebellion comes decisions that are careless, impulsive, and often lead to regret. If you choose to be inflexible to have things your way, make sure you make it happen in a productive and calm way versus one that is rash and rebellious.

**ADDICTION.** Addicts as a group have endured a great deal of chaos in their own and their family lives. When it comes to the point that they've lost everything, or "hit bottom," they are usually desperate to find a way to regain control. Many recovering addicts think that by becoming extremely rigid in their habits they will gain control over their addictions and their lives. And they do—but the tradeoff is a loss of opportunities, relaxation, connections, and openness with people. That said, when it comes to being rigid about staying away from your addiction, rigidity is the way to go!

**ONCE BURNED.** Sometimes those who have undergone a significant, painful, and often unwanted change, milestone, or trauma—such as divorce or the loss of a close friend—refer to the process of recovering as pulling themselves up by the bootstraps. In the aftermath of the trauma is when this person may go too far—start laying down rules and becoming overly rigid. "I'm never going to date anyone again who doesn't get along with his parents." "I'm not going to take a job that requires me to stay late ever again." They live by the words "never again . . ." whatever it might be.

This might lead to people's making such radical choices as never dating again, never marrying again, never making another close friend again, or never going back to work. Because of their baggage, they begin to put up walls, becoming far less flexible and more closed up. As soon as they see what they consider even a small warning sign in the form of a similarity to what they remember enduring before, they stick to their now hard-and-fast rule of being completely closed off to that possibility. Self-protection is good . . . but remember, it's all about balance. Don't miss out on the good, because you were burned by someone or something bad.

**Now that we have an idea where the need to be rigid arose, I** want to illustrate to you how flexibility affects every area of your life.

## Work

Are you someone who is always worrying and fretting about something along the lines of: how can I get out of that new and daunting task at work?

Work is one of the most important areas where we must all learn to be more flexible. Think about professional athletes. Yes, many specialize in a certain position such as quarterback or pitcher, but scouts are always looking for team players who are flexible, somebody they can move around and who will excel at different positions. They want to utilize these people in different ways as the team's demands change.

In economic times like these, it becomes more important than ever to be flexible. If your department has budget cuts and you don't have other skills and tools, you may be in a vulnerable position. We talked in the coping chapter about options, and how grown ups are always careful to have options and backup plans when it comes to their careers. One of the biggest pitfalls here is lack of flexibility. If you lack the skills and tools or education to be flexible in your job, look into acquiring what you need to overcome that issue. Don't be shortsighted and unwilling to try new things, volunteer, or give more than is asked for at your job. I mean, if you were the boss, wouldn't you want a utility player who is open to new and different tasks that can better the business?

I once knew a brilliant fifth-grade teacher—let's call her Mrs. Thomas. Mrs. Thomas's students were the most well-behaved and best-educated students in the entire school district. She herself was a favorite, much loved by parents, teachers, and her students alike. She ran a tight ship but was very loving as well. She had a rigid plan about the most successful way to teach her kids, and she followed it to the letter year after year, class after class. Her students knew from talking to former students that in the fall they would be writing reports on historical subjects, the entire winter season would be spent on writing skills, and spring would bring an intense focus on scientific happenings from the past and present. It was very helpful if your older sister or brother had taken her class, because you knew exactly what was coming and what was expected of you in full detail!

One year, much to Mrs. Thomas's shock, the school decided to change her grade assignment and assigned her to teach the first grade. After fifteen years of teaching the same curriculum over and over, handling a classroom of seven-year-olds was something that she was not prepared to do, let alone had ever considered. Mrs. Thomas had a rigid personality, and this change threw her into a tailspin. The woman who had led the pack and been the absolute role model as an outstanding teacher fell into a full-blown state of depression due to this major change and her inability to be flexible and adapt to it.

Now you are likely feeling sympathy for her—as did I, because no one wants to be forced into a sudden, dramatic change like that after all those years of comfortable routine. However, I am sharing this story with you to highlight the significance of the need to be able to bend without breaking at work. Sometimes life deals you a card that you don't like. You have to demonstrate coping skills and flexibility to know how to trade that card in or manage the one you were dealt so you can keep playing and hopefully win the game! Yes, even when you were dealt the worst possible card!

## Parenting

I realized the moment my first newborn daughter was crying uncontrollably even though she was dry, fed, and not tired that my ability to control her behavior was out the window. Parenting is a job for those with the skills of a grown up—or it will make you a grown up in a hurry!—and it most certainly involves flexibility. The only sure thing all new parents discover about a baby is that everything about this child and its behavior is unpredictable. Babies cry for no reason. They are always soothed by being taken for a car ride—until one day they aren't. One day they take the bottle happily; the next day they angrily reject it. Just when you think you've figured them out, they throw something new into the mix for you to scramble to find answers for.

As a child grows and his individual personality starts to assert itself, he will demonstrate personality traits, interests, and habits that seemingly come out of nowhere. Parenthood is one long, humbling process of learning to read signs, adapt, and be flexible enough to best meet the needs of this unique child while not torturing yourself. Striking this balance is a tremendous challenge and daily evolving process. Those of us who have the strength of being flexible adapt the most quickly, have the least stress, and, strangely enough, end up with the most flexible and adaptable children.

## Romantic and Personal Relationships

In terms of marriage and dating relationships, if both partners are rigid in the same ways, things can run smoothly, but if you're both rigid in opposing ways, say hello to conflict! Let's say you are a clean freak in the sense of hygiene, germs, and cleanliness but don't mind clutter and papers strewn all over the place; your partner can't stand the clutter but doesn't get hung up on cleanliness. Imagine the endless daily battles, which can escalate into major problems if you can't find common ground.

Or what if your partner is set in his ways about arriving on time, but you think the world should wait until you can arrive? Do you always arrive in separate cars at different times? Being flexible not only will lessen your conflicts, it will offer you the ability to compromise and connect with the person you care about.

I once counseled a couple who had been married for three months when they came to my office for help. We will call them Derek and Stephanie. Before meeting Stephanie, Derek enjoyed what he called "boys night out" every Friday night. He and his friends had been doing this since college, and the tradition had continued to the present day. Derek, Stephanie, and the friends were all about thirty years old. When he met Stephanie, Derek made it crystal clear to her that this was the way he spent his Friday nights and it would continue until the end of time—no matter what happened in their relationship or how serious they got.

You see, as I mentioned in the intimate-relationships chapter, people tell you who they are when you meet them, and Derek told Stephanie that he was a guy who needed and insisted upon his Friday nights with the boys. It will not surprise you that Stephanie was hoping he'd show some flexibility when it came to that particular Friday-night activity. She went so far early on in their relationship as to ask him things like: What if there were an important work function she had to go to? What if it were her birthday? Or better yet, what if they were married and she was giving birth on a Friday night? Would he be with her then? Derek's answer in every case? "I'll be with the boys!"

(Note: If you are wondering what I might have said to Stephanie if she had consulted with me before getting married, I would have let her know that if she planned to share a future with him, she had better learn to be okay with his inflexibility on this issue and she'd also better be finding something else to do on Friday nights. If she couldn't do both of those, I'd tell her she should find someone who was less attached to his boys nights out.) Now, why were they in my office? Stephanie was hoping that once they actually got married, he'd change (see the discussion of fantasy voice in the intimate-relationships chapter), and she wanted me to convince him that he should. Derek agreed to come because he wanted me to get her to stop nagging him every Friday and let him go out in peace.

I am sharing this story with you in hopes you see the challenges that come up when people in romantic relationships take a stand and refuse to bend. Stephanie and Derek broke up four months after their $30,000 wedding. Stephanie ended the marriage but was absolutely devastated. Derek's take on the whole thing? "See why I stick with my boys? They'd never leave me if I wanted to spend one set night a week with her!"

## When the Rest of the World Won't Bend

Let's talk a bit more about bumping up against another person's rigidity, which is a very common problem in people's lives—though hopefully not as extreme as Stephanie's! This might happen when somebody you've dated once or twice is considering having a relationship with you. Or when somebody is pondering the decision whether or not to hire you. Maybe you're not their usual type to date, or have an unusual background and skill set that is not tailor-made for the position. Maybe you've been trying for decades to please a rigid, overly demanding spouse. What does it feel like when you come up against their rigid rules and expectations?

It's usually quite frustrating and disappointing. It's important for us all to keep in mind how we react when running into brick walls (if only so we don't do it to other people). What about when a friend, boss, or romantic partner says to you, "This is just the way I am and how I do things. You're going to have to accept it"? Sometimes it can be a motivator that makes you want to fight more and try harder to make the other person see things your way. It can also make you give up and retreat.

A rubber band is a good metaphor for human flexibility and what can happen when trying to accommodate overly rigid people. You can stretch it quite far over and over, but if you stretch it too hard, it will eventually snap and break or just wear out and lose its elasticity. People can reach both those points. I've given, I've given, I've given, and now I've had enough . . . and SNAP! I lash out in anger, yell, scream, and throw a major tantrum. Or, I've given, I've given, I've given, and now I'm completely exhausted and worn out and have nothing left to give. I become quiet, resigned, and listless.

Have you reached either of these points? Remember, when inflexibility says to you, *take it or leave it*, it is saying, *I don't care what you think or want. What I want matters more than anything.* And you, when faced with this attitude, do have a choice. You don't have to take it; you can most certainly leave it. I'm not saying that would necessarily be easy or convenient, but it is always an option. Understand and remember this—now *that* is truly empowering.

## A Challenge to You

I saved flexibility for the final chapter of this book, because my whole intent along this journey is ultimately to challenge you to be flexible. I hope that I have encouraged you to examine who you truly are and what you want out of life and have shown you that being a fully loaded grown up is a very desirable thing. Hopefully you are considering that there are areas you might want to change and are exploring options to conduct your life a little differently while adapting more peacefully to its difficulties. If you have been working the chapters, then you have been working flexibility to the 100 percent level. You already have the skills and tools in place, and your life will most certainly change as more and different opportunities will open up to you.

You and I have now spent a lot of time together on your journey through this book. Hopefully you've learned more about how to be a grown up and to fill your life with a balance of fun, freedom, and responsibility. My goal with my clients is to be a strong member of their support group and help them grow and change for as long as that process takes. I am there to offer support, guidance, and tools for change for an hour a week until we reach our goals, and then our work is done. In this case, within the pages of a book, our work together is now complete.

The remaining work toward improving your life rests in the power of you. You are now armed with knowing yourself better. You have a greater understanding of who you are, where you have come from, and your strengths and weaknesses. You have new tools in your toolbox to help you face the challenges in your life and maximize your potential. Now that you know all the secrets of how to be a grown up, the rest is up to you. Do the work to better your life, and grab the moments you have and make them as happy, productive, and fulfilling as possible in every area. You're worth it!

# Conclusion

# N ow what?

I am guessing that the reason you picked up this book in the first place was because you knew your life could be more fulfilling or you felt you were facing challenges for which you lacked the right tools or information to overcome. At the beginning of this book, you took a quiz. Your original score may have clearly shown that you had major difficulties and issues in one or two specific areas, or maybe that your life would benefit from some minor shoring up in all the categories, or any combination thereof. Whatever your score, you should now be much more aware about which areas you'd like to work on in order to build the life you long to have.

Just as this book now rests in your hands, the power to apply this new self-awareness and the tools for growth lie solely in your hands as well. Like any journey, there will be bumps in the road, slipups, times you'll need to relax and recharge your battery, and times when you just want to throw your hands up in the air, give up, and abandon the whole process. We all have those moments, or even days and weeks of these moments. That's normal and to be expected on a lifelong journey. Just as a diet is not just changing how you eat for a month or two, becoming a fully loaded grown up is about maintaining consistent progress for the rest of your life.

Again, you are the only person who lives with you 24/7, 365 days a year. You know the details of your finances, what your priorities and passions are, what types of friends you are drawn to, and whether you prefer to drown your sorrows in a tub of ice cream or a good book. To that end, I am convinced that you can be your own best champion, provided you are willing to engage yourself in your own life and follow my suggestions in this conclusion.

To be honest, I wish I could come along with you and help you out whenever you need it. You know, give you that encouragement to get started, prod you when you're tired, throw out some advice along the way, and push you when we both know you need that shove to go in a particular direction or to work a little harder. When times were really tough for me, I often wished I had someone right there to coach or counsel me when I needed some guidance, an ear to listen, or a push to go do the right thing for myself. Most of my clients have said the same thing.

But since I can't do that, here I will outline for you how best to get going and take the first steps to begin to change. Then we'll talk about the mental motivation and emotional endurance to keep going even during those times when you feel you can't do it any longer. It's time to rally the troops—the troop of you, of course—and begin to take action toward changing your life *for the better!*

## Positive Action

You are likely already familiar with the power of positive thinking, and I personally believe that there is great importance in the theory and practice of it. There have been countless studies about how a positive attitude affects those facing serious medical conditions and treatment and how it benefits their outcome and physical well-being. Many medical and psychological professionals preach the importance of positive thinking to reduce stress, depression, and anxiety, and there is research to back up this approach. In addition to positive thinking, I'm sure you've seen or heard about the literally thousands of books and articles out there on the power of positive intent, the law of attraction, getting what you want by surrounding yourself with positive people, and using focused and affirmative words and thought.

All of this is good, especially if it improves your physical, emotional, or psychological well-being. If you are a believer in the power of positive thinking, I encourage you to continue investing energy in that area. If you do not subscribe to that type of thinking, that's not a tremendous problem when it comes to the path toward being a fully loaded grown up. Although consistently negative thinking isn't good for anyone, I know many successful, fully loaded grown ups of both personality types—believers and nonbelievers.

When it comes to creating optimum success and having the life you want, you can read every book in the world on how to improve yourself, and you can talk to every expert. You can spend hours pondering how to best tackle your problems and days basking in the sensation of what it will feel like to reach the glory of success. You can embrace the power of positive thinking to help you feel motivated and uplifted, you can work the law of attraction on a daily basis and write down endless plans, goals, and outcomes. You can do all these things without ever leaving your house—and without ever seeing any appreciable results! That's because, in spite of how influential and powerful all of that can be, it is still missing the critical element needed to actually change your life. That critical element is *positive action*.

Positive action is the ability to take ownership of your life and take steps toward making change and moving forward. Our thoughts, emotions, and attitudes are important and can absolutely impact our ability to change and grow, but we must actually put all of these aside if they get in the way of taking action and moving forward to get things done. I cannot tell you how often I have thought my desk was a mess and how many feelings I have had about that mess. I hate the fact that I cannot find anything when there is clutter. I am often irritated and angry not just about the pile of papers themselves, but about how long it takes me to find anything when I need to work on something right away. I could write pages and pages about my thoughts and feelings about my disorganized desk. I could launch into a monologue about them in a car, on a plane and across the country, however, until I actually take action—make a plan and get cleaning and sorting, my desk will never be the neat and orderly place that I am hoping for.

This need for action spills over way beyond the example of a disorganized desk and into every area of life. You can have thoughts and feelings about a new job, losing weight, seeing an old friend, paying your taxes or even re-creating your life from top to bottom, but until you actually move to action and take the necessary steps, nothing will get accomplished. Sounds simple, right? Well, the concept is simple but it's the actual doing and creating new habits that stick that becomes the challenge. The weight-loss industry alone makes billions of dollars every year based on the reality that we can buy a book or fitness gadget, pay for a program, or be handed a plan and at least make a start. But most of us cannot continue to maintain taking action long enough to keep the pounds off for our lifetime (or even a year)—so, guess what? We turn to another book, plan, or program in hopes that it will inspire us to get moving again.

What keeps us from taking action? Something we have talked about a great deal throughout this book—emotions and how they get in our way. Negative emotions like fear, anger, sadness, and shame could all potentially be at the core of why you find it hard to take action. But, to make improvements in your life, you must begin taking positive action no matter what feelings you are experiencing.

## Getting and Staying Motivated

Getting motivated requires focus. Focus toward who and where you are, who and where you want to be, and a commitment to take the steps, even baby ones, that connect these two. Whatever the reason or reasons were that brought you to where you are now, today is the day to commit to having positive experiences more often. Think about who you want to be in a month, a year, a decade. What is your ideal dream goal? When you are much older, say ninety years old, what do you want to look back on and know you've accomplished? Make a list of each of the ten areas in this book. Next to each area, write down your ultimate goal to accomplish. Ask yourself what your ultimate prize is, and begin to think about how great it would feel to have it happen. These desires can keep you directed as you go through tough times, keep you working toward your goal, make you persevere when it seems you're not getting anywhere, and most important, keep you focused.

Of course, slipups and backsliding along the way are inevitable and are what often can cause us to lose motivation. We all have bad days, some we can control and some we cannot. We all have our moments when we are working hard toward a goal and then have an off day. Maybe you're tired, overworked, under pressure, feeling burdened, or just don't have what it takes in the moment to keep pressing on. Then there are the days when maybe you are doing all you can, working hard, and trying your best to grow and change, and life throws you a curve ball. Maybe you just had a fight with a friend or your mate, your job or relationship is in jeopardy, or you suddenly had the roof leak in your home and are scrambling to save your furniture from getting ruined. Change and growth don't come in a straight line. Two steps forward, one step back will still take you where you want to go! In the quest for being a fully loaded grown up, you are looking for progress, not perfection. If you slip up or slide back or have to sidestep, that's not only okay, it's to be expected. Just refocus and resume what you were doing before the difficulty started.

## Getting Unstuck

Feeling stuck in the outside world is an experience we can all relate to. Whether we're stuck in traffic, in a relationship, at a party we feel we can't leave, or with a project or task we didn't feel like taking on, we all know the discomfort that feeling stuck can bring. But what happens when the stuck feeling is happening in your inside world? The world that is your mind, that place that no one else sees or hears about unless you let them?

Inner stuckness creates those negative voices in your head that say things like, *I don't know where to begin, this is too hard, I'm too overwhelmed, I've tried this before and failed,* and leave us unable or unwilling to take positive action. Interestingly enough, it's not those voices that keep us stuck, because we can use positive self-talk to counteract those voices and say things like: *I can do this, I've never tried it this way before, I have never been this motivated, I am excited about new possibilities and a greater life.* It is our *responses* to those voices that keep us stuck. Most people have one of two negative reactions. Either they avoid and withdraw, or they lash out. Whichever the response, the end result is the inability to take action and thus the inability to grow and change your life.

Withdrawing and avoiding are unproductive because they pull you directly out of the game that is your life. Whether you fully disengage and stop playing completely or avoid issues and challenges, they both keep you from taking charge and control of your progress. If your life were a car and you were the driver, this means you either got out of the car completely or started driving blindfolded or with your hands periodically over your eyes. The end result: either you don't move at all or you move haphazardly and then crash unexpectedly because you were avoiding looking where you were going.

I had a client—we will call her Erin—who came to see me when she found herself overwhelmed by some legitimate problems. She was recently separated because her husband left her for another woman, and she had a significant amount of debt. She had a long-term stable job as a paralegal. She had several close friends, but if you asked her, those were the only two things going really well in her life (and I had to agree—if she took the quiz at the beginning of the book, career and support system would be the only areas where she truly had success). Before Erin came to see me, she was withdrawing further and further from the world and her problems. She stayed home, turned off her telephone, refused to check e-mail and sat in bed eating cinnamon rolls all day (her favorite). Since the sudden breakup of her marriage, Erin had missed thirty-five out of fifty work days, had not spoken to any of her friends, and in that two months she had gained fifteen pounds and hadn't even realized it.

Erin's avoidance and withdrawal from her life had her headed directly down a path of even greater destruction. She was being warned by her supervisor that she would soon lose her job, and her friends were becoming disgusted and impatient by her lack of contact. Erin's report to me was that the loss of her marriage and her mounting debt were so overwhelming that on most days she felt only enough energy to call in sick to work and then spent the rest of the day on the couch or in bed, eating. She spent much of the day crying, sleeping, and eating. If Erin had only done the bare minimum of maintaining the friends and job she had, she would have still at least had two out of the ten areas in this book covered. Had she begun to take even small steps toward any of the other eight categories, she would have had something to work for that was positive and growth oriented.

The lashing-out phenomenon can be directed toward the self or others. When it is directed at the self, this reaction involves everything from self-criticism to internal verbal abuse to self-sabotage. This is a destructive scenario because you, the person you're with 24/7 and can never escape from, is bashing you and beating you up—talk about stuck! You can't walk away, and you can't hide, because, as the saying goes, wherever you go, there you are. Self-abuse is damaging because if you don't have you on your side, who do you have? Add to it that the toughest foe is the person who makes it the hardest for you to find strength. Do not make that foe you, and do not deplete your strength by fighting with yourself. If you do, you will impact your ability to take positive action because you will be exhausted and worn out, and your self-esteem will have been impacted by the constant barrage of criticism.

Laura was an attractive single woman who had fallen into the bad habit of staying out late and drinking until all hours of the night. She started going out because sitting at home reminded her how lonely she was and how much she hated being single. Each night she would come home from work, look in the mirror, tell herself how unattractive she was, throw on sweatpants, and go out to the local restaurant for a few drinks. At the restaurant, she would tell the other frequent customers all the reasons she thought she was alone. They would try to convince her otherwise, she would cry, and then she'd go home. Many mornings she was exhausted from crying and being out late, so she'd leave for work late and arrive at the office looking drawn and worn out. People would ask her what was wrong, and she'd launch into a monologue about how she was alone, no one wanted her, and how she'd never be married. After about a year of this cycle, Laura came to me because she felt completely isolated.

She reported that she hadn't had a date in years, that the regulars at her local bar/restaurant seemed annoyed at her, and that even her friends at work were beginning to pull away. She told me her confidence was shot and that she was beginning to feel a sense of despair. Laura did indeed struggle when it came to dating, but her constant self-abuse had made her stop caring about her appearance, impacted her job because she was always late, and left her friends and those around her tired of hearing her complain and criticize herself nonstop.

Once I got Laura to put the bat down and be kinder to herself, she began to take positive action in regard to her appearance, her job, and her friendships. Guess what? She ended up marrying the owner of the restaurant who later said he "never noticed her before, and then one day, she just had this sparkle." The "sparkle" came once she began to take positive action and like herself.

## How to Initiate Positive Action

- **LEVERAGE.** If your current situation and circumstances are far from your ideal grown-up life, let me offer you some encouragement. You are not starting at zero. Everyone has at least one area where they shine. The idea is to leverage that strength to shore up your weaker spots. In what areas are you already fully confident? Even if it's just one, let that be your springboard. Erin, the woman I mentioned above, is a good example of the use of leverage. Erin had always been strong in the career and support-system categories, so we knew that she clearly had good skills in those areas before her emotional derailment. I had Erin work on rebuilding the career and friendship categories first, so she could begin to regain some confidence, and then we handled the issues around money and intimate relationships. This enabled her to rely on the good things in her life in order to get through this painful time. In the end, her strengths—a long-term job and the sincere care and concern from her friends—were there to help.

- **REMIND YOURSELF THAT IT'S YOUR LIFE.** You're in charge, and any growth and change will come out of your taking ownership of your life and your commitment to making it better. If you have tried to lose weight or stop a bad habit, for example, to please someone else, it's doubtful you succeeded for long. If you have attempted to make a change before you were ready and/or able, I would imagine it was hard to keep it going. I'm sure you get the idea here—you have to want to make a change and be ready to take positive action. You may not be able to go back and change the past, but you certainly can do things differently in the present and the future.

- **FOCUS.** Even if it's for two minutes a day! Turn off your phone and computer. Breathe. Visualize. Center yourself. Do whatever it is that you do to concentrate your attention on something important. Zero in on the issues and challenges in your life, and make your plan for addressing them that day.

• **BABY STEPS.** What if making a list doesn't help, but only discourages you because it seems so overwhelming? What if the challenge before you seems too large? What if the work you need to do could take months or even years to accomplish? Make yourself choose one small task, a baby step, one small change, because even small changes will impact your success.

 Taking small steps, accomplishing small goals, and the resulting confidence lead in a continuous loop to taking bolder steps and bigger risks, continued increasing confidence, and eventually the establishment of a better life.

•**VALUE ANY PROGRESS.** It's like starting a diet. You may want to lose three pounds every week, but if you wind up losing just one, it's still moving in the right direction. It's the first step in the journey toward losing fifty. Don't fall into the trap of becoming discouraged for not losing (or doing or accomplishing) enough. Any progress at all is a great change!

• **FACE THE BIG PROBLEMS HEAD ON.** Now, if you have a pressing problem that urgently needs to be addressed, one that is affecting every area of your life, I would suggest that you begin there. The more pressing issues can start a domino effect into areas that were once strong, or it can further damage areas that were initially weak. Give it your best shot and focus on fixing that challenge piece by piece, step by step, issue by issue.

- **MOVE THE DIALOGUE INSIDE YOUR HEAD TOWARD THE POSITIVE.** Embrace your past successes, and keep your eye firmly on the future of having more. As life changes, so will your specific challenges. Marriage, having a child, getting a promotion, divorcing, moving, losing a job . . . in the years to come you will no doubt be both rewarded and tested in every area. The advantage of being a fully loaded grown up is being able to ride the waves of change bringing forth your new abilities and skills.

- **DO IT ANYWAY.** No matter how bad you feel, how depressed or anxious you might be, or how unfair your circumstances seem, nothing will change until you take positive action to change it. Take that step forward even if you have to carry your negative feelings and worries along with you. Their weight will lessen as you do something positive and productive anyway.

- **TAKE A BREAK.** Even the most diligent and responsible person needs a day off. If you are tired, overloaded, and need a break, take one! But then get back on task toward pursuing your goals.

- **WITH MAINTENANCE COMES BIG REWARDS.** If your life is reasonably in order and you are handling things in an efficient and productive way, it's less costly in every way to go off and have a great time. When your household, family, job, or business is under control, you can go off for a vacation with a free mind. If your weight and appearance are consistently maintained, you can splurge for a couple of weeks and eat whatever you want without guilt! If you've been saving your money or have worked hard for extra income, you can indulge in buying something extra without financial stress.

You have finally reached the end of this book. If you have thought about yourself and how you'd like to improve your life, then you're already walking down the path of being a grown up, and you should be proud of yourself. Throw in balancing your responsibilities with fun and freedom and you will be exactly where you need to be. With that, I wish you good luck and great success. Thank you for letting me be part of your journey toward becoming a fully loaded grown up.

*Emotional Vampires: Dealing with People Who Drain You Dry* by Albert J. Bernstein

*Codependent No More: How to Stop Controlling Others and Start Caring for Yourself* by Melody Beattie

*Toxic Coworkers: How to Deal with Dysfunctional People on the Job* by Alan A. Cavaiola and Neil J. Lavender

*The Pathfinder: How to Choose or Change Your Career for a Lifetime of Satisfaction and Success* by Nicholas Lore

*No Excuses! The Fitness Workout* by Harvey Walden IV

*No Fat Chicks: How Big Business Profits by Making Women Hate Their Bodies—And How to Fight Back* by Terry Poulton

*Body Traps: Breaking the Binds That Keep You from Feeling Good About Your Body* by Judith Rodin

Any addiction book by Janet Woititz

Alcoholics Anonymous books

*Intuitive Eating: A Revolutionary Program That Works* by Evelyn Tribole and Elyse Resch

*Breaking Free from Emotional Eating* by Geneen Roth

*To Buy or Not to Buy: Why We Overshop and How to Stop* by April Benson

*Please Understand Me: Character and Temperament Types* by David Keirsey and Marilyn Bates

*Passionate Marriage: Keeping Love and Intimacy Alive in Committed Relationships* by David Schnarch

*He's Just Not That Into You: The No-Excuses Truth to Understanding Guys* by Greg Behrendt and Liz Tuccillo

*It's Called a Break Up Because It's Broken: The Smart Girl's Break-Up Buddy* by Greg Behrendt and Amiira Ruotola-Behrendt

*Couple Skills: Making Your Relationship Work* by Matthew McKay, Patrick Fanning, and Kim Paleg

*Getting the Love You Want: A Guide for Couples, 20th Anniversary Edition* by Harville Hendrix

*Keeping the Love You Find: A Personal Guide* by Harville Hendrix

*The Dance of Intimacy: A Woman's Guide to Courageous Acts of Change in Key Relationships* by Harriet Lerner

Any book by Peter Walsh on clutter

*Getting Things Done: The Art of Stress-Free Productivity* by David Allen

*Emotional Freedom: Liberate Yourself from Negative Emotions and Transform Your Life* by Judith Orloff

*The Seven Habits of Highly Effective People* by Stephen Covey

*How to Win Friends and Influence People* by Dale Carnegie

*Influencer: The Power to Change Anything* by Kerry Patterson, Joseph Grenny, David Maxfield, Ron McMillan, and Al Switzler

*Crucial Conversations: Tools for Talking When Stakes Are High* by Kerry Patterson, Joseph Grenny, Ron McMillan, and Al Switzler

*The Total Money Makeover: A Proven Plan for Financial Fitness* by Dave Ramsey

Any Suze Orman book

*Toxic Parents: Overcoming Their Hurtful Legacy and Reclaiming Your Life* by Susan Forward and Craig Buck

*Facing Love Addiction—Giving Yourself the Power to Change the Way You Love* by Pia Mellody

*Couple Skills: Making Your Relationship Work,* by Matthew McKay, Patrick Fanning, and Kim Paleg, 2nd ed.

*I Don't Have to Make Everything All Better: Six Practical Principles That Empower Others to Solve Their Own Problems While Enriching Your Relationship* by Gary Lundberg and Joy Lundberg

# ACKNOWLEDGMENTS

**It takes a village to write a book.** There is no way I could have completed this without the support, dedication, talent, and brilliance of an incredible group of people. I thank you all from the bottom of my heart. I hope that you get everything that you work for and hope for in your lives.

My daughters Jordan and Katie, I love you with all of my heart. I hope this book and the time we spend together helps you continue to grow and change in wonderful and unique ways. You are both responsible, fun, and very special. You make me proud.

To Mom and Dad, thank you for always giving me the guidance I needed and for being supportive and available at a moment's notice. You live your lives with kind hearts, wisdom, and a passion to help others. Thank you for being such wonderful role models.

To my grandma, Selma Kalt, you accepted and loved me unconditionally no matter what. I know you are with me every day, even though you are no longer here.

Julie McCarron, thank you for an incredible introduction that led to me having this book. Your brilliance and creativity are endless, and I appreciate how you have cared enough to work your mind and fingers to the bone. Your editing skills are extraordinary, and I am blessed to call you a friend.

Suzanne Wickham, thank you for investing your belief, time, and energy into me and my writing. I am grateful for your introduction to HarperCollins; this has been a life-changing experience. I know that working with you means that I am in great hands.

Nancy Hancock, thank you for your ability to balance warmth and enthusiasm with solid constructive criticism and guidance. You are one hard working, highly intelligent editor and a real grown up! Words cannot express how grateful I am to have had the chance to work with you. Thank you for everything.

The entire team at HarperOne, thank you for your time and talent. What an incredible group of people you all are!

Greg Behrendt, you are a tremendous talent, incredible friend, and an inspiration. I thank you for everything you've done to support me both personally and professionally. I look at your and Amiira's relationship in awe. You are such an amazing example of a relationship that has the foundation for lasting love. Your ability to prioritize your happiness and the needs of your family are impressive and admirable. I feel blessed to know you both.

For helping to create a fantastic book cover: Joan Allen (photographer extraordinaire), Jan Ping (no one makes my hair and makeup look so good while also being an amazing friend), Cary Fetman (fantastic wardrobe talent and you made me laugh too).

To Dougall Fraser, thank you for teaching me the ins and outs of writing a book, for introducing me to the wonderful Julie, and for never-ending advice and support. You are a true friend, and this book would never be this book without you. I adore you and David.

Kevin and Rikki Fortson, you say you had little to do with my career in the media, but you two started the ball rolling, and for that I am forever thankful. Everyone should be so lucky to have incredible friends like the two of you. Thank you for everything you do for me and my family.

Melissa Burnstine, Leda Knee Guine, Rikki Fortson, Tali Kaplan, Michelle Poe, Wynn Helms—thank you for your creative brilliance and for being a sounding board when I needed it most.

Mark Lesser, thank you for helping me battle the challenges and celebrate the victories. You taught me that even trees sometimes need something to lean on, and for that I am forever grateful.

To my mentor Gloria Hirsch, you told me that I had the foundation to help others and filled me with your wisdom about children and grown ups. Your passing was too soon, but your legacy lives on in all who you taught and touched.

Dan Black, you have been there for me from the beginning, helping to shape my career and offer me guidance and wisdom. I am grateful to have an attorney with a huge heart and tremendous intelligence.

Ra Kumar, thank you for being my agent and for seeing potential and possibilities in me, even before I knew they were there myself.

Rona Menashe, you are an incredible publicist, visionary, and protector. Thank you for your never-ending support and dedication.

There are many wonderful and talented people who have made an impact on this book and my career. There are a few who deserve special mention and thanks: Howard and Robin Borim, thank you for your creative ideas, video talents, editing, lending of your home, and friendship. Earl Nicholson, you are an amazing makeup artist, stylist and friend—how I look today has so much to do with your influence. Jan Ping—incredible hairdresser, makeup artist, and friend—I love that we can fly together. Stephen Guine, thank you for keeping the world up-to-date on my career with your web talents. Lastly, to all of my family and friends who have done everything from lending an ear to driving my children, please know that I could never have written this book or even manage my life without you. Thank you for always being there.

**Stacy Kaiser** is a licensed psychotherapist, relationship expert, media personality, and body language expert. She has worked with thousands of individuals, couples, and families for the last twenty years through her private practice and corporate consulting and on television. Her philosophy for growth and change emphasizes being honest with yourself and others, and taking responsibility for your thoughts, feelings, and actions. She believes with the right techniques, guidance, and support anyone can make lasting changes. Since 1994 she has also worked with corporations, public institutions, government agencies, and philanthropic organizations including assisting the FBI with communication skills and the Los Angeles Fire Department with tools to counsel people after 9/11. Stacy has made over 100 television appearances in the last year. She is Access Hollywood's resident Body Language Expert and has counseled people on Tyra Banks's, Greg Behrendt's and Larry Elder's nationally syndicated talk shows as well as on *The Real Housewives of Orange County*, VH1's *Celebrity Fit Club*, and Lifetime's *Diet Tribe*. She has gained a reputation for helping people face the truth that is holding them back from leading a life filled with a generous balance of responsibility, fun, and freedom. She lives in Los Angeles with her two daughters.